A way marker on the Via Francigena

f life came with such clear-cut instructions, we wouldn't need to undertake pilgrimage, and what fun would that would be?

Other books by Ryan Tandler

Walking to Santiago: A How-To Guide for the Novice Camino de Santiago Pilgrim

Almost Half of Me: My Journey to Losing 125 Pounds with Sleeve Gastrectomy

Acknowledgements

Thank you, Marty and Kevin, for always being there for me. Thank you, family, for listening to me talk endlessly about the Via for so many months before and after my trip. Thank you, parents, for sending me to good schools. Thank you, teachers, who taught me how to write.

Thank you, Rick Steves, for your excellent television and guidebook series, which make traveling to Europe so easy and enjoyable.

And thank you, readers, for giving this book a chance.

To Readers and Pilgrims

The challenge in writing a travel and how–to book is that the information you need is constantly changing, and there's a lot of it to know. I update this book every year with new information and things I've learned, and it's a daunting task, particularly as technology changes year to year. I've done my best to make sure that the information contained here is accurate and that it is up–to–date as of publication.

The most useful thing in updating this book every year, aside from what I learn on every new pilgrimage, is hearing from readers. Reviews left on Amazon or on web forums help me know what information is most useful to you and what else I can include to make this book more relevant and helpful to pilgrims. So if you can and are so inclined, please take a moment to leave a rating or review on Amazon or on a Camino or Via Francigena forum. It helps me, and it helps our fellow pilgrims, and it helps me help our fellow pilgrims.

Buona Via!

Table of Contents

Who is this book for?

The Via Francigena is for everyone, and so is this book. Many who walk the Via are experienced travelers, pilgrims, and hikers, and many are not. No matter. While some of the information in this book may be familiar to you, much of it may not, and I wanted to make this information useful to as many people as possible.

Similarly, some of the contents of this book may be more familiar to Europeans than North Americans. As this book is targeted to the widest audience possible, I encourage readers to focus on the information most useful to them.

Part I

The Via Francigena

Introduction

The routine of backpacking is simple. Every day is pretty much like the day that came before it: you wake up, you walk, you eat breakfast, you walk, you eat lunch, you walk, you eat dinner, you sleep, you wake up, and you walk again. The venue determines whether you get to shower at the end of the day or wash clothes, whether you have to pitch a tent, whether you're cooking over a fire or dining at a trailside café, but the essential activities of backpacking are always the same. Whether you're doing it for six months or a week, it doesn't change. That's the basis for this book. Whether you're walking the entire Via or just a section, all pilgrims have the same needs.

The idea for this predecessor to this book, **Walking to Santiago**, came to me one day as I was walking a section of the Katy Trail in St. Charles, Missouri. The Katy Trail used to be a rail bed and is made of crushed, white stone, so on that July day, even though it was fairly early, the heat radiating from the path had me turning around after a short 3.5 miles. I was carrying about 50 pounds and sucking down plenty of water, but the heat and humidity were winning as the sun got higher. As I walked, to keep my mind off of the heat I considered everything I had learned about backpacking over the last several years as it became my favorite hobby.

When I was preparing for my first pilgrimage, on the Camino de Santiago, I read everything I could find on the subject, and as I read, and especially as I re-read, I was perturbed by the lack of detail in some books claiming to be the definitive how-to on the Camino. "Take a lightweight backpack." Gee, what inspired advice!

In other cases, the advice is downright bad, if not dangerous. "Use a needle to puncture a blister." Wow, food for thought as a doctor is telling you in Italian that your foot is infected and you need to go home.

What needs to be added to the literature of the modern pilgrimage is detailed advice from a backpacker. Advice like how to pick out a backpack *and* how to use the thing; why you should use trekking poles; and how to properly treat a blister.

I'm no expert on the entire Via Francigena. Neither am I an expert backpacker in the vein of those who have walked the entire Appalachian Trail or the Pacific Crest Trail. I can't offer you detailed information on all the villages you'll pass through or the elevation gain and loss, and I can't regale you with advice learned while traversing thousands of miles on America's longest trails.

Instead I offer you my advice as a Camino and Via veteran and as someone who spends many a weekend out on the trail somewhere. I regularly take day hikes and do short overnights, carrying just The Ten Essentials or several days' worth of supplies. In learning to hike and in making my pilgrimages, I made mistakes, I sought advice from others, I read every Camino and Via guide and narrative and how-to I could find, and I learned. That's what this book is: detailed backpacking advice learned the hard way and applied to the Tuscan section of Via Francigena.

This book is based on my personal experience of walking the Tuscan section of the Via Francigena from Lucca southward, but much of the information here – particularly relating to general travel to and within Europe and on gear selection – applies to the entire Via. It is by no means the definitive book on the subject, I am no means an expert, and I encourage you to read all you can about the journey before you go so that you can make the best-informed choices for yourself.

With my experience and mistakes in mind, I offer you this guide to the Via Francigena that I hope will prove useful to you, and especially to novice hikers taking on this great and meaningful undertaking.

1. A brief history of the Via Francigena

"You are Peter, and upon this rock I will build my church."
(Mathew 16:18). This play on words in the original Greek of the Bible
(*Petrus* is "Peter", *Petra* is "rock") is the scriptural basis for the primacy
of Rome in the Catholic Church. Peter's exact position among the
apostles is a matter of some debate, but he is commonly seen as the
leading apostle, vested with, in the same chapter of the Book of
Mathew, the keys to the kingdom of heaven. It's for this reason most
depictions of Peter show him carrying a key. In the wake of the
crucifixion, as the apostles spread out from Jerusalem to spread the
Gospel, Peter traveled to Rome, heart of the western world at the time,
to evangelize. Peter's descendants, the Bishops of Rome, more
commonly known as the popes, have led the Roman Catholic Church
ever since.

Sometime between AD 64 and 68, Peter was arrested, tried, and
condemned to death for his proselytizing. Sentenced to be crucified,
Peter demanded he be crucified upside down, declaring that he was
not fit to suffer the same form of martyrdom as Christ. The execution
was carried out in the center of what was a race course on the Vatican
Hill of Rome. Peter's followers removed and buried Peter's body not far
away, and ever since, pilgrims have traveled to his tomb to pay homage
and to pray to God in the presence of the Prince of the Apostles.

Today the basilica that stands above the tomb of Peter is
inarguably the greatest architectural achievement of western man,
designed and built by men whose genius remains unrivaled –
Bramante, Michelangelo, Maderno, Bernini. It is the center of Vatican
City, the smallest sovereign state in the world but the religious capital
of almost 1.3 billion people, making it by far the largest denomination
of the largest religion in the world.

The Via Francigena – The Road from France – became the main
pilgrimage route to Rome during the middle ages. Those medieval
pilgrims began their journey at their own doorstep, traveling to the Via

and down the Italian peninsula. But by custom, the route of the Via Francigena begins in Canterbury, England. It crosses the English Channel, continues through eastern France into Switzerland, goes up and over the Alps, and down the center of Italy to Rome.

It is historical coincidence that Canterbury is considered the starting point of the Via. Around 990 CE, Sigeric the Serious, Bishop of Canterbury, travelled to Rome to receive his pallium, a church vestment once given to important church officials to symbolize the authority vested in them by the Pope. Among Sigeric's party was a scribe who recorded their daily itinerary, and this document survived. Only because it survived is Sigeric's route considered the official route.

In 1985, an Italian archaeologist named Giovanni Caselli, who specializes in ancient roads, retraced Sigeric's journey, and in 1994 the Council of Europe declared the Via a European Cultural Route. And then nothing happened.

For comparison, the Camino de Santiago network was made a European Cultural Route in 1987. That year, 2,905 pilgrims reached Santiago and claimed their compostela. That number is now above 300,000 annually. The internet, so far as I can find, has no record of how many pilgrims reached St. Peter's Basilica from the Via, but one unsourced figure puts the number at 1,200 in 2012. Another says about 25,000 people walk the Via each year, but not all the way to Rome and not all as pilgrims.

A few factors explain why the Via has yet to achieve the popularity of the Camino. First, it's twice as long, at 1,056 miles, and so takes twice as long to walk. Second, because it takes longer to walk, the Via is more expensive. Third, the terrain is more variable, and crossing the Alps on the path itself cannot be done in winter. This also means the Via is a more solitary undertaking. Far fewer pilgrims spread over a much greater distance means the trail is less pilgrim-dense. It changes the nature of the journey, with much less comradery and much more time for silent contemplation. Depending on what you want out of your pilgrimage, this solitude is either a drawback or an advantage.

I don't expect this to last. The Via is too beautiful, its destination too awe inspiring, the cultures and cuisines through which it passes too seductive for pilgrims to stay away. Regional and local governments have seen the opportunity the Via presents. Looking across the continent to the Camino, they see the euros and vibrancy pilgrims bring to northern Spain, and they are taking steps to make the Via accessible to pilgrims.

The Tuscan government, already adept at attracting tourism, has jumped into this endeavor with gusto, re-routing the Via to minimize road walking and erecting way markers. As the trail becomes more accessible and more pilgrims travel to the Via, many of them Camino veterans like myself, the pilgrim infrastructure – the hostels, the bars, the public fountains – will catch up, attracting yet more pilgrims.

2. Why pilgrimage?

Every person must discover for themselves where they belong, and to discover this, one must first discover who they are. We want to be ourselves, but we also want to be part of something larger than ourselves. That is what pilgrimage is for.

The pilgrim is transient. He owns little. He controls his time. He has few needs. Because he has few needs, he is more free to be himself, and when he engages with others, it is because he chooses to rather than needs to. The engagement is more genuine, more organic, less transactional as a result. Under these circumstances, the pilgrim has the freedom from his own wants and those of others to learn who he is and then to be that person.

But pilgrimage is not hermitage. By definition, it is not walking away from something but toward something. And others have done it, too. Pilgrims are a community nested within larger communities. Pilgrimage is a chance to be a part of those communities even as you contemplate what community you want to belong to. It's a safety net, a safe place to be now while you figure out where you want to be forever.

On my pilgrimages, I've got the sense talking to many pilgrims that they were searching for something greater than themselves on their trek. This aspect of the Via, related to but less appreciated than the Catholic underpinnings of the ritual, is its humanism.

Modern life, particularly in North America, is isolating. Some speak of loneliness as an epidemic. We just don't connect with people anymore; there is less a sense of community. A lot of people blame this on technology, and while that plays a role, sociologists noted this shift in western culture well before the Internet and mobile devices became commonplace. People give too much emphasis to unfounded nostalgia, but in general, the sense of community that prevailed for most of human history – the sense that we are all in this together, from raising our kids to participating in global affairs – isn't what it used to be. Where once it was difficult for a person to disavow their community and for their community to disavow them, it's easy today to decide that you are no longer a part of your community, and it's easy for communities to decide who is and isn't a member. At the same time, it's harder to connect and to join in meaningful ways.

Cause and consequence of this change is that we have fewer and fewer rituals. Rituals are something that communities design and participate in; as the community evolves, so too does the ritual. Rituals help to ground people: "It's harvest time, we're having a harvest festival, and I will contribute to it and participate in it because I am a member of this community." Individuals have rituals too: "It's a weekday morning, and before I deal with anyone else's problems, I'm enjoying this cup of coffee because in this community of one, that's how we start our day."

Pilgrimage is a ritual, and like all rituals, it's grounded in a succession of communities: the pilgrim community, the European community, the Western community, the Christian community, the Human community. So much of our lives today is about defining ourselves in ways that capture just one part of who we are. To my mind, the underappreciated humanistic aspect of the pilgrimage ritual is to say: "I'm Ryan, and I'm walking this road because I am a member of the community of the human race like all who came before me and will follow me." It's a ritual that captures its participants in their totality in a way that little else does.

When we think back upon the millions of pilgrims who have walked the Via, they are anonymous to us, but we recognize, however faintly, that they were human beings who belonged somewhere, and by their undertaking they became part of a collective history. By walking the road, we declare that we too are human beings, and we too belong somewhere, and we become part of that history.

In a time when it's easier to decide where we don't belong, it's a wonderful moment in life when we can decide where we do belong.

Walking is a perfect medium for pilgrimage. When you're hiking, you're only doing the one thing. When I'm on the trail, I can disconnect. In an age where you're expected to be reachable by email and cellphone all the time, the trail is where I'm unreachable. I can't get enough of that feeling. A lot of people say that on a long-distance hike is the freest they ever feel. Even on a day hike, for a few short hours of a random Sunday, the only thing that matters is me taking myself up over the next hill and down the other side, and it matters because I decided that it matters. Tomorrow other things will matter again, but right now, it's just my backpack, the trail, and me. For me, hiking is a mental release as much as a physical one.

Beside the solitude of the hike, the exertion facilitates thought. The rhythm of your own steps, the slowness of travel, the feel of the ground under your feet. It all forces us to notice our bodies, as much a part of understanding who we are as our minds and souls.

And with the exertion comes the low-grade suffering of hard work. I believe that at the root of the human condition is our desire to be comfortable because we mistake comfort for happiness. We want nice things, and we don't want to be uncomfortable. This desire dictates too much of our lives, from the jobs we choose to how we spend, or waste, our time. Diogenes knew this, so when all he owned was a bowl to collect the coins he begged, he threw the bowl away so he would no longer fear losing it. Saint Francis knew this, so when he came to the point in his life when he had to choose between the path of comfort his earthly father's money provided and the path of saintliness his heavenly Father offered, he stripped off his fine clothes and embraced the life of a mendicant.

Hiking long distances is not comfortable. Muscles ache, blisters form, feet hurt. For me, it focuses the mind. The world shrinks down to just me, the ground, and my aching feet. It's the closest my mind ever comes to being both awake and silent. It's meditation. It's why I enjoy a long hike but don't take the same degree of pleasure in a short hike.

And that hard work gives way to accomplishment. Overcoming the discomfort to arrive at your goal makes attaining that goal so much sweeter. It's just more satisfying. It's why people run marathons and do triathlons. And after all that hard work, you appreciate the small pleasures more: a hot shower, a soft bed, a decent meal.

My first day on the Via was also my longest of that trip, and because I was in good shape, I didn't prepare for my hike at all. It was

18 miles on rolling terrain. Around mile 16 I stopped in the shell of an old building to answer nature's call and then leaned against the wall for a moment. I was tired; I was jetlagged. I could see the hill town where I was heading, meaning the last two miles would be steep. I had gone through the daily cycle of pilgrimage: bouncing out the door in the morning, enjoying the scenery, getting lost in my own thoughts, minor ache turning to minor pain, and now just wanting to get where I was going.

Imagine how good it felt to get there.

Part II

Logistics of the Tuscan Via

3. Traveling to and from the Via

When to go

For most people, the unfortunate answer to the question *When should you go on the Via* is *Whenever you have the time*. If you do have a choice, then here are some things to consider.

The summer months are peak tourist season generally as well as the busiest and hottest months of the year on the Via. Transportation and hotels will be more expensive, and traditional sights and the Via will be more crowded. On the upside, all the accommodations are open. On the downside, they're at capacity. Tuscany's tourism industry makes it one of the busiest regions of Italy in the summer, and you'll be competing with tourists for space in many of the more popular towns. That said, the summer months are also when the most pilgrim-only accommodations are open. Finally, some people do choose to camp on the Via, and the summer, while hot, is also fairly dry.

April, May, September, and October are the shoulder season months. These are less crowed and less expensive. The weather is especially excellent in the fall, even into late October. I consider this an ideal time to go, as the weather is more pleasant than the summer months, most accommodations are still open, and it's a little less crowded. If you're interested in either observing or participating, grapes in Tuscany are harvested in late September and olives in early November, and many villages hold festivals to celebrate the fruits of the season. Some agriturismi let guests help with the harvest.

November, December, January, February, and March are the off-season. This is the cheapest and least crowded time of year to go, but the weather can be cold and wet, and because there is less pilgrim traffic, many accommodations shut down for the season. In addition, the cold temperatures require a little more gear, and thus add to the cost. But because these are the off-season months, airfare, train tickets, and accommodation prices can be lower than in the peak and shoulder seasons, so the expense of additional gear may be a wash.

Flying to Europe

The internet has made flying to Europe easy. Gone are the days when you needed a travel agent. Go to any ticket broker site (like Travelocity, Expedia, etc.) or direct to an airline's site, or shop on a broker site and buy on an airline's site. It's easy and fast. One good travel tip for flying anywhere: if you book through the airline rather than a broker, you may have an easier time making any changes to your itinerary or getting upgrades.

It's important for North Americans to remember when making all of your arrangements that most flights land in Europe the day AFTER you take off, so if you leave on Thursday you arrive on Friday. You may think it's obvious, but people do make that mistake.

Jet lag is real but perhaps overblown. At least some folks are more susceptible to it than others, but you can fight it, and staying active is the best way to fight jet lag. After you land and get settled, go for a walk. Fresh air and sunshine are the best remedies for jet lag, as is staying hydrated. My goal on my first day is to go to bed between 9:00 and 10:00 after a nearly full day of activity.

A flight from the US to Europe costs from $1,100 to $1,800 dollars for an economy seat and can take from seven to twelve hours depending on where you take off from and where you land.

The seats on transatlantic flights are a bit larger than on a domestic flight, and on the newer planes there's a TV screen built into the seat in front of you with a menu of movies, and there's often a USB outlet to charge your devices. Most people don't like flying, but transatlantic flights are not as bad as you may think.

It takes a lot of frequent flyer miles to fly to Europe, but if you have them and have some flexibility, it saves you a lot of money. The catch is that flying with miles limits your travel dates and destinations. Of course, business and first class cost more miles, but they limit you in other ways too. Here's how:

- A rewards flight costs a certain number of miles, but that number changes depending on the date. It will cost more miles to fly on a Friday or Saturday than on a Thursday or Monday.

Similarly, flights in peak seasons or near holidays cost more miles.

- Not all flights have seats for rewards travel, so if you see a flight you like, it might not be available to you. The flights that are available tend to be less desirable. For instance, you want the 2:20pm to your connection city to shorten your layover, but the available awards flight leaves at 6:00am, turning your short layover into a day of sitting in an airport wishing you were a tree.
- Rewards flights tend to go only to major airports. For instance, at least on American Airlines (and partners), you can't fly into or out of Venice on miles. Even major tourist cities and national capitals may not be reachable via miles. I found out that American Airlines doesn't have rewards flights into Lisbon, Santiago de Compostela, or Ljubljana, at least the last time I checked.
- You can't pay for part of a flight in miles and the rest in cash anymore. It's one or the other. Perhaps you are close to your rewards ticket. You can buy more miles, or a friend can gift them to you, but with that comes a hefty fee (the more miles, the more dollars). I looked into it once and found that buying some additional miles and transferring some from a friend would have cost more than paying cash *and* would have limited my travel options to boot.

I've flown to Europe on miles twice and saved a lot of money doing it. It made my plans more flexible, even allowing me to change my destination only two weeks in advance with no fees. You can check a bag for free, board in Group 1, and are more likely to get an upgrade. If you fly a lot for business, it's a great deal: the company or client reimburses you for the flight, but you get the perks and miles. Some people despise miles programs; I've had good experiences.

The class upgrades that you can purchase are generally not useable on international flights, but it never hurts to ask for an upgrade just because (the worst they can say is no). Call the airline a few weeks before your flight and ask, and again a day before you leave. You can ask at the airport, but I've found that unless you are a Platinum Power Ranger Awards Member, you won't get one at the gate. I asked for an upgrade once, and the woman at the gate apologetically told me it would cost another $3,200 dollars. I replied that that wasn't an upgrade: it's buying a more expensive ticket. But from my seat in coach I could at least see the much more comfortable seats in first class that recline completely flat.

Choose your seats carefully. Some of the features that seem nice on a domestic flight can be worse on a transatlantic flight. For instance, an exit or bulkhead seat's tray table is stored in the arm of the seat, which gives you less room side-to-side and makes the tray a tight fit if you're a bigger person. The window seat in an exit row is colder, and while it may okay for a couple hours, you might get uncomfortable beyond that. You can look up the best seats on a given aircraft at various websites, including **seatguru.com**.

When booking your flights, pay attention to how long your layovers are. Some of them can be very long, and some of them can be so short that you'll have a hard time making it to your next flight, especially in large airports where the gates may be far apart, if you have to change terminals, and yes, even if you have to change airports (which does happen in cities with multiple airports, such as New York).

You will have to go through customs on your way home, something to keep in mind if you're checking any luggage and your connection is tight.

Should you schedule some time for traditional sightseeing?

Yes! If you have the time and money. I'm of the opinion that if you're flying all the way to Europe, you'd be foolish not to spend at least one day doing some traditional sightseeing. I'm a lover of European art, history and culture, so it doesn't take much for me to come up with an excuse to spend a day seeing major sights. If you take your pilgrim's mindset to the major cities, you can do it cheaply, too:

walk instead of using taxis or public transit, and stay in hostels (they're not just for students anymore).

Coming from the US or UK, chances are that to get to a smaller city, like Lucca or Siena, you'll have to catch a train from Florence, Pisa, or Rome. Consider taking a day to enjoy those cities' sights before heading for the Via, or choose any other city you can get a cheap flight out of to your destination.

Also keep in mind that when you're in Tuscany you're traveling through a region that has been occupied by sophisticated cultures for thousands of years. The Via probably has more world heritage sights per mile than any trail in the world. It passes through some major cities, but even in the small villages there are churches and villas filled with world-class art. The small town you stop in may once have been the seat of a powerful family, and that family may have commissioned a renaissance master to fresco the local church. Stick your head in everywhere you go. Remember that the journey isn't just about arriving at your destination and that time is the one thing you have in abundance on the trip.

Getting to the Via in Tuscany

Getting to the Via is not complicated. Italy is compact, has a good rail and bus system, and the Via passes through mid-sized cities. Tuscany is most easily accessed through Rome, Florence, or Pisa. It's easy to fly into any of these cities' airports and catch a train or bus to your starting point, and its relatively inexpensive. Some common starting points in Tuscany are Lucca and Siena, two of the larger towns in the region that in their heyday competed with Florence for feudal supremacy (they lost). This section – from Lucca to Siena – is one of the most popular portions of the Via in Tuscany and laces together several noteworthy towns worth seeing.

Lucca is west of Florence, and typically getting there means taking a bus or regional train from Florence's main station. A number of other towns along the Via are located along the same train line. Lucca's claim to fame is its defensive wall. Three miles around, it's wide enough in spots for full-sized restaurants on top, and it's a great promenade to see the city and watch Italians going about their day.

Siena is south of Lucca and can be accessed through Florence or Rome by bus or train. From Rome, a bus is can be direct, including one daily (as of 2018) leaving straight from Fiumicino airport in Rome. Getting there by train means changing trains in Florence, which is less convenient and takes longer. Siena's claim to fame is everything about it. The city's prominence is owed to its being on the Via. The Via made Siena wealthy because the pilgrims meant trade and the route was an artery of commerce in the middle ages. The Piazza del Campo, the city hall and the cathedral (*duomo*) are must-sees. The *duomo* contains a number of artworks by renaissance masters, including a room by Pinturicchio. Another must-see sight for pilgrims is Santa Maria della Scala, which served as a hostel and hospital for pilgrims, among other functions, for centuries and is now a museum covering the building itself, art from the region (including modern), and local archaeology. Every inch of it is worth seeing. It's across the square from the cathedral.

Note that major cities often have more than one train station and bus station. For that matter, they can have more than one airport. Sometimes these stations and airports are quite a way from the city center. When purchasing tickets, making connections, and booking accommodations, be sure you're leaving from and going to the right station.

The biggest issue you may have is a transportation strike, but these are scheduled in advance with lots of public notice, the trains still run during rush hour, and the strikes sometimes last only a few hours.

Another oddity of the Italian train system is you have to validate your ticket before you board, unlike in most other countries. After you purchase the ticket, look for a machine on the platform. Just slide your ticket into the machine to validate it.

Don't rule out busses. They are cheaper than trains and often more direct.

Remember that Rome and Florence are not far apart by train, so if you find a cheaper flight to one or the other, both are good options to fly into. Along the Via, busses make for convenient transportation for skipping sections or taking side trips.

Money on the Via

Cash is king on the Via and for tourists in general. I'm no different than most in that I use my credit and debit cards for almost every purchase at home, no matter how small. There's more than enough tourist trade in Tuscany that most places accept credit cards, but every place accepts cash, and there are no foreign transaction fees for it. It's not uncommon for hotels and restaurants that do accept credit cards to charge an additional fee for it in addition to the exchange rate. The credit card system is also different in Europe, and you'll need to know your pin, if you don't already (that's right – credit cards have pins like debit cards, and that's what they use in Europe instead of signing receipts). Using cash makes things so much easier.

As of this writing, 1 euro is approximately $1.14. A quick Google search can give you the latest conversion rate.

No smart traveler uses traveler's checks anymore. There are fees to get them, fees to cash them, and the hassle and time of waiting to get and cash them.

In addition, anyone changing money is also making money. Whether it's a bank, ATM, or a store, they charge a little for themselves in the transaction, or offer a lower exchange rate and pocket the difference. This rate is less in Europe than at home.

Don't bother getting euros before your trip. Banks, especially in the US, and stores in Europe charge more than ATMs to change money, so use ATMs. The ATM is my first stop in the airport after I get my luggage.

You can use a debit card or a credit card to get cash from an ATM. With a debit card, you will pay a flat transaction fee, a few dollars, that doesn't get higher even if you take out more money. You can minimize these fees by minimizing your trips to the ATM, which means taking out the maximum amount your bank will allow. You will need your pin to withdraw money, so memorize it in advance and *don't* write it down and stick it in your wallet.

If you withdraw cash from an ATM using your credit card, your bank will treat the transaction as a cash advance, a short-term loan which comes with a high interest rate. Using your debit card just withdraws your money from your bank account, so there is no interest. If your checking account does not have a debit card attached to it, get one before you go to Europe and memorize the pin. Treat ATM withdrawals from your credit card as an emergency option only.

Europe uses the chip-and-pin type of credit and debit cards. These cards, instead of a magnetic strip, have a microchip embedded in them, and instead of signing the receipt, you enter your pin number. Most new cards issued in the U.S. now have a chip and pin, but we don't enter the pin to make purchases; we still sign receipts. Nonetheless, your credit card does have a pin, and you should memorize it before your trip.

If you don't have a chip card (your bank will issue you one for free) or it isn't working, in most places in Europe, you can still use your magnetic strip card, and if you have a problem using one at an ATM or kiosk (such as in a train station), the teller or ticket agent at the counter can run your card for you.

Before you travel, call your credit card companies and/or bank to let them know where you'll be traveling and when. Be sure to include any place you have a layover. This prevents the bank or credit card company's system from thinking your transactions are fraudulent and stopping them. If your card throws up a red flag, you'll need to call the bank to unlock your card, and that's a real pain when you're calling from Europe, especially if you don't have your phone set to call in Europe. Avoid even the chance of that happening – call ahead before you leave the US. When you do, find out what the daily or transaction maximum is for withdrawing cash using your debt card, and request that it be increased if you think you'll need to withdraw more. You can also ask for an increase in your credit limit from your credit card company. Note that some banks treat the weekend as a single day, so the daily withdrawal limit will apply to the entire weekend.

Use calling your bank as a reminder to get on the State Department's website and register your travel. In the (very) unlikely event of an issue wherever it is you're traveling, the nearest consulate or embassy will know you're there and won't forget you when the helicopters are pulling folks off the roof.

The Via is as expensive as you want it to be. If you make use of the pilgrim hostels in churches and monasteries, it's probably the cheapest trip you will ever take other than camping. Twenty-five euros a day can be more than sufficient depending on where you sleep and what you eat. If you stay in hotels or agriturismi, and if you eat at more expensive restaurants, of course you'll spend more money. Tuscany can be very expensive if you want it to be (and there's nothing wrong with that!).

I take my debit card and two credit cards. Two credit cards might be considered overkill by some, but I like the mental security of having a backup, and some places won't accept certain brands of credit or debit card. In addition, I take $150 of American cash as a true emergency fund.

It used to be good advice to know the location of a Western Union in case you needed someone to wire you money. Now with peer-to-peer money transfers, this is as simple as an app or visit to a website, including Western Union's but also PayPal, Facebook, Venmo and Apple Pay.

The worst happens and your money belt, along with your passport, cash, credit card, and debit card, is lost or stolen. Don't panic. Start by canceling your credit and debit cards, then get to a US consulate or embassy. They will be able to get you a new passport and will give you a short-term loan to get you back on your feet. Your general European travel guidebook should contain more information on this unlikely problem.

On the last day of your trip, you don't have to spend all the euros you have left. Major airports, like the one you're probably flying into to get home or have a layover in, have currency exchange shops that will turn your euros back into dollars. Often these are in the domestic as well as international terminals. Yes, you will lose a little in the transaction, but dollars are more valuable than the chintzy souvenirs you only bought just to spend the money. Or just save the euros for your next trip.

The language barrier

In general, you never have a difficult time finding someone who speaks a little English in Tuscany. It's the *lingua franca* of the tourist trade. Some people speak it better than others, but it's very easy to get what you need.

But you are passing through a lot of small towns that don't see many tourists, and you may find a shopkeeper, hotelier or waitress who doesn't speak any English at all. Seriously, having someone ramble on at me in Italian even after I've said (in Italian) that I don't speak Italian was an eye-opening experience. It's instant appreciation for what non-English speakers go through when talking to us (for instance, you'll find that no matter how slowly someone speaks in a foreign language, it still sounds very fast to you, which doesn't matter because you don't understand it at any speed).

As a rule, though, if you're interacting with someone who doesn't speak English, chances are it's obvious that person knows what you want. For instance, you walk into a *gelateria*; you're more than halfway there in telling the proprietor what it is you want just by coming through the door. You just need to fill in the details, and you only need a few phrases for that. And I don't use this example lightly: gelato is serious business. My Italian is miniscule to non-existent in quantity and quality, but I can pronounce my preferred gelato flavor like an native speaker.

You will be doing only a few things on the Via: walking, eating, and sleeping. You don't need to know the whole language to manage those, but it is helpful and polite to learn a handful of words in Italian. Remember that you are in their country; they are doing you a favor by speaking in English, so return the favor by learning the Italian phrases you're most likely to use.

Start a conversation by asking if the person you're talking to speaks English (ask them in their language!). If they say no, try to speak in the native language of whomever you're talking to. Sometimes after a few words, they'll start trying out their limited (or sometimes not so limited) English to help you out.

If they do speak English, speak slowly, annunciate, avoid colloquial language, and don't use idioms.

If they don't speak English, do your best in their language. If someone can speak grammatically incorrect, poorly pronounced English and be understood by English speakers, you can do the same in Italian.

Gestures work. Pointing works. Sometimes writing something down or drawing a picture works. Do whatever you need to do to communicate, and don't be embarrassed. It's all part of the experience. You can even fall back on technology as there are apps that translate for you even if you're not online, including Google Translate.

Most importantly, your mother was 100% correct when she told you that you can get almost anything you need in life with *"per favore"* and *"grazie."*

Measurements, numbers, and time on the Via

Italy uses the metric system, the Celsius scale and the twenty-four-hour clock. All three are easy to master.

For measuring weight, the metric system uses grams. There are one thousand grams in a kilogram (kilo). One kilogram is 2.2 pounds, so half a kilo is about one pound, a quarter kilo is about half a pound, etc. One hundred grams of lunchmeat is a little less than a quarter pound, or a decent sandwich.

For measuring volume, the metric system uses liters. One liter is approximately 34 ounces, so a 32-ounce Nalgene bottle is about one liter, half a liter is about 16 ounces, two liters is about 64 ounces, and 4 liters is approximately a gallon. One liter of water weighs 1 kilogram (how many pounds is that? 2.2).

For measuring long distance, the metric system uses kilometers. One kilometer is about 0.6 miles, give or take. Five kilometers is about three miles. To do a quick conversion from kilometers to miles, divide the kilometers by half and then add back ten percent of the original (e.g., 1 kilometer divided by 2 is 0.5; 10% of 1 is 0.1; 0.5 plus 0.1 is 0.6, the number of miles in a kilometer). You may find as you hike that kilometers are a little easier to judge than miles.

For temperature, Europeans uses the Celsius scale. The actual conversion from Celsius to Fahrenheit is to divide the Celsius temperature by 5, then multiply by 9, then add 32. To ballpark the conversion from Celsius to Fahrenheit, just double the Celsius and add 30. So, 20 degrees Celsius is 70 degrees Fahrenheit, a comfortable day.

Decimals are different in Europe. Instead of a period, they use a comma. So whereas a euro and a half for us is €1.50, in Europe it's €1,50. By the same token, whereas we would put a comma in a four-digit number (there are 5,280 feet in a mile), in Europe they use a decimal (there are 5.280 feet in a mile).

In Europe, the first floor of a building is the ground floor, and what we call the second floor is the first floor.

The twenty-four-hour clock (better known as the military clock in the U.S.) is easy to use. Any time before 1:00pm is the same as on the twelve-hour clock, except between midnight and 1:00am. For instance, 12:30am is expressed as 00:30. Any time after 12:59pm, just add 12. So 1:00pm becomes 13:00, 5:30pm becomes 17:30, etcetera.

Returning from the Via

Rome or Florence are both good options for flying home. Depending on where you end your walk, you can catch a bus or train to either city. If you go to the station, they will advise you on your best option, though the web, especially sites like **Rome2Rio.com**, are making it easier than ever to figure out transportation options in small towns. If you'll be ending your pilgrimage in a smaller town, it's best to figure this out in advance as they have less frequent bus or train service.

Hiring guide companies

It is entirely possible for any person in reasonable shape, at any age, to walk the Via independently and even solo. Hundreds of people do so every year. You also have the option of hiring a guide company for either a guided tour or for a self–guided tour.

In either case, the guide company will make the logistical arrangements for you. In the case of a guided tour, this typically includes transporting your luggage from hotel to hotel, so you hike with just a daypack. Your guide will know (or at least should know) the history of the places you are passing through and will have some expertise in religion, art, and architecture to enrich your experience. You will most likely travel with a group, and these groups can be either completely *ad hoc*, or they can be arranged around a common trait (seniors, for instance) or interest (religion).

Self–guided tours include booking your accommodations and can also include arranging your dinners, luggage transport, and transfers to your starting point and to the nearest airport at the end of your pilgrimage. A good self-guided tour company will also provide you with directions and a 24/7 help line should you need any assistance. There are quite a few companies offering these services. I've personally used **Camino Ways** and been pleased with them.

Whether you hire a guide company or not, you can hire a service (if one is locally available, and there usually is), to transport your bag to your next hotel or hostel. You (or the service) can call ahead to the hotel or hostel. If you do this, it's important to take a daypack so that you can carry the essentials (extra socks, first aid kit, water, etcetera).

I've done pilgrimages independently and as self-guided tours, and I've enjoyed both equally. They are each simple in their own way, and what I sacrificed in spontaneity by having accommodations booked in advance I feel I made up for in convenience. I ate better on the self-guided trips, enjoyed a good breakfast every morning, and took a few extra comforts I don't take when I travel unsupported. That term – supported and unsupported – is a good way to think of what self-guided tours are. In long-distance hiking, an unsupported hiker carries everything with her; a supported hiker has someone who meets them at designated points, every couple of days if not every day, with food and water and usually takes them to a hotel for the night, then drops them off again in the morning. At the end of the hike, both the supported and unsupported hikers had different but equally impressive and enjoyable experiences.

I've not done a guided pilgrimage, but I also think they're a great way to make your trek (anyway you do it is a great way). Tour groups can be excellent travel, offer (hopefully) good company, and a good guide can create an incredible experience for guests by providing historical, artistic, and religious insights about the areas the Via passes through.

About sending your backpack ahead. Some people consider this cheating. I don't. First, for people who may not be able to carry a pack, sending their luggage ahead enables them to do the Via, and however you do it, the Via is worth doing and is an accomplishment to be unabashedly proud of. Second, the weight of a backpack is not the primary source of discomfort on a long-distance hike; the distance is. Carrying *yourself* is the real challenge, physically and mentally, because you are the heaviest thing you are bringing along. If you need to send your pack ahead, or just want to, do it and be confident that you are still a pilgrim.

There's no shortage of those obsessed with their own version of what constitutes an authentic pilgrimage, which typically includes any or all of these: start at the furthest terminus of your route, carry all your gear yourself, stay in hostels, don't use electronics. I've come to hate the word "authenticity" and its derivatives as just the latest buzz word passed down to us through lifestyle bloggers and jaded image managers. In the case of pilgrimage, these criteria would limit the Via to those with no physical or temporal limitations, but the Via is for everybody, whether you have a week or a year to do it, or whether you have some physical disability or limitation or not, or whether you just want the trip to be a little more convenient. *Your* pilgrimage is *your* authentic experience, period. Own it, love it, be proud of it, repeat if desired.

4. The daily Via

What I like about hiking is how singular it is. In our modern lives, it seems we rarely have the chance to focus on just one thing, but when I'm out on the trail, my world shrinks down to my immediate surroundings and my body. After the first few miles, I fall into a rhythm and just keep going. I imagine myself as the Energizer Bunny, moving slowly but inexorably forward, confident that my feet will take me all the places I wish to go. It is a source of pleasure and confidence and security.

The activity of hiking and the daily routine of long distance hiking have that in common. It's about repetition, and somehow while most repetitive tasks in our lives bore us and make us feel trapped, the repetitions of the hike make us feel free.

Even on long hikes that turn into forced marches, the pain I sometimes experience becomes its own Zen task: my world shrinks down even more, until it is just me and the pain. A lot of people will never understand it, but I think Jon Krakauer said it best in his book about the 1996 Everest disaster:

> "People who don't climb mountains...tend to assume that the sport is a reckless, Dionysian pursuit of ever escalating thrills. But the notion that climbers are merely adrenaline junkies chasing a righteous fix is a fallacy...Above the comforts of Base Camp...the ratio of misery to pleasure was greater by an order of magnitude than any other mountain I'd been on...And in subjecting ourselves to week after week of toil, tedium, and suffering, it struck me that most of us were probably seeking, above all else, something like a state of grace."

Of course, what Krakauer was doing up on Everest is a whole different animal, but hiking is like any other physical undertaking, by turns exhilarating and exhausting. Read any memoir of a long-distance hiker, and you'll find that most of them at some point compare the task of long distance hiking to a job. It is not all warm days, cool breezes, and fields of wildflowers; some days it is mud and cold and stubbed toes. When I think back on my Via journey and all my days on the trail, I think I cherish the hard days most, for I felt a greater sense of accomplishment at the end of them.

What time should you start hiking every day?

What time do you want/need to start hiking every day is the better question. Hostels generally ask guests to leave by 8am so they can start cleaning up for the next group of pilgrims, so expect to leave your hostel no later than 8. If you're in a hotel, you probably have until 10. Whether you start hiking or spend more time lingering over breakfast is up to you, but there are some things to consider.

First, how fast do you hike? You should have a general idea based on your practice hikes. Personally, I'm a very slow hiker.

Second, when do you want to arrive? One of my favorite things about the Via is not needing to know this answer to a certainty. The answer *When I get there* is liberating. But even if you don't know exactly when or where, having a ballpark helps.

I know I'm a slow hiker, and I know that I like to arrive in the early part of the afternoon so I can spend it napping, having lunch, doing chores, and exploring, so I usually leave before 9:00.

On the trail

You'll find that many pilgrims like to get a few miles under their belt before stopping for breakfast. Cafes along the Via can be busy in the morning, mostly with locals. You're not on a schedule! Try to linger. I've found that people are especially sociable in the morning.

Most daily Via guidebooks break down the Via into 15- to 18-mile segments, though some are longer and some are shorter. You can make any day longer or shorter, though, as you pass through villages where you can cut a day short, or hike on a little further to the next village. Good guidebooks list all of these villages.

The path itself

Tuscany is defined by its hills: the towns are usually on the top of the most prominent hills, the villages and farms are scattered between. If you keep to the most common stage breakdowns, every day follows a similar routine.

Chances are you stayed in the old part of town last night. When you leave in the morning, you'll walk through town, typically passing through the newer part of town where most people actually live. There's traffic and not always sidewalks. Eventually you're out of the town-proper, and you're in what we would call a suburb. You're walking on the main road, and there's no sidewalk. Small hatchbacks fly by you at what seem homicidal speeds; not all drivers swing wide for you. You're walking downhill.

Finally, after several kilometers, the Via turns away from the main road onto a side road, often a gravel road. There's a lot less traffic and a lot more farms. If you turn around, you'll see the towers of the town you just came from, up on its hill and standing out against the skyline. You may have some large ridges and hills to cross, but the Via switchbacks up and down them rather than going straight up or down, which makes it easier. The trail follows the curve of these ridges for lone distances, so you are frequently on the crest, which means less up and but more exposure to wind.

The hills are steep, but once you get up on them, you have incredible views. Your bus group tourists would kill their seatmate for these views! Vineyards, olive groves, plowed fields, Tuscan farmhouses, the occasional village or church. It spreads out around you like someone set out to create the perfect pastoral landscape. If you find yourself on top of tower in a town looking down on the surrounding countryside, you are allowed to look at the tourists who drove there and smugly think, *'You're seeing the hills from the tower, but I saw the tower from the hills.'* Just don't say it out loud.

At the end of the day, when you're most tired, you probably have to walk uphill again, because that's where your destination for the day is. The large towns are on hills. It's the morning in reverse, and you'll pass through suburbs and probably walk on a paved road the last couple miles until suddenly you're in the old town, often after passing through a medieval wall.

The actual pathway varies. Paved roads are more common than many would like. Gravel and crushed stone are most common. Dirt paths through the forest are less frequent. I find that no surface is more comfortable to walk on than God's own dirt and wish there was much more of it. Most hikers average two-and-a-half to three-and-a-half miles per hour during the course of a 15-mile hike over varied terrain.

It may seem at times like you're in the middle of nowhere, but chances are you're on someone's farm. The Via cuts through fields on farm roads, my favorite being the one through a vineyard a few miles south of San Gimignano. If you stop and turn around, you have a great view of the towers in the distance. You'll also walk through neighborhoods just like yours at home, though most driveways are gated. Forest-path hiking is pretty rare in Tuscany as so much of the land is put to agricultural use, and the region is densely populated, like most of Italy.

Navigating the Via is pretty easy. Signs and pilgrim emblems are everywhere on the Tuscan Via. It is possible to take a wrong turn, but it's hard to stay lost, as you won't see any signs or emblems. Turn around and backtrack, look at the map in your guidebook, read the route description, or ask a local to direct you back to the path.

There are several sources now for GPS maps that integrate with various walking, running, and cycling apps to provide you with exact directions on the Via. The Via in Tuscany is well marked enough to not make it necessary, but these GPS apps do give you a nice peace of mind.

How your hike goes depends largely on your likes and dislikes. Sometimes you'll hike with other people, sometimes you won't. Some people listen to music on the Via, some don't. Some take a camera, some don't. There's no right way to do the Via, and that's the point: you get to do it entirely your way.

Arriving at your destination

Whether you stop for lunch is more dependent on what time you get started and what time you intend to arrive at your destination. I like to stop for the day around two in the afternoon, so I skip lunch on the trail or take something small with me. Many restaurants in smaller towns close from about 2:00 until dinner time, not unlike the Spanish siesta. This is especially true on Sundays, when even grocery stores may not be open in the afternoon. Plan accordingly.

If you don't have a reservation, I recommend scoping out accommodations as soon as you arrive at your destination. Ask fellow pilgrims, refer to your guidebook, go to the tourist office, or just look for signs. If one is full, another is probably a few doors further down the street. However, if you are going to be in a town popular with tourists, call ahead even in the winter. If you're planning on staying in a pilgrim hostel, call ahead; do not assume there will be a second hostel open to you. These are too few and too small to make that assumption.

If you're staying in a hostel, after getting your pilgrim passport stamped at the front desk and turning over a few euros, pick a bed in the dorm or go to your assigned room. Resist the temptation to take a nap. In fact, if you can avoid it, don't even sit down, lest you find a you-shaped sweat stain on the sheets when you get back up. Shower stalls and hot water can be in short supply (lo, how much we suffer), so I suggest grabbing your shower kit and cleaning up as soon as you can.

Once you're clean, I suggest doing your laundry (more on this later). Sometimes there's a sink inside, other times outside, but get this chore out of the way early so that everything dries before you go to bed.

If you're in a hotel, you most likely have a private bathroom and can do your laundry in there (and clean up after yourself). Most hotels will also stamp pilgrim passports, as will some bars and tourist information offices. Hotels in Italy will make a photocopy of your actual passport, so don't be surprised or worried if they ask you to leave it with them for a bit.

Finally, do whatever it is you want to do next. This is my favorite part of the day: after a long hike, I'm clean and relaxed, with my aching feet propped up on a chair, a bottle of wine on the table, and a parade of people to keep me entertained. This is an excellent time to keep a journal.

After a nap, it's fun to wander around the town, looking for interesting sights, old friends, and new friends. Before you know it, it's dinner time.

Evenings

If you're in a busy pilgrim town inhigh season, it can be difficult to have dinner by yourself, and that's a good thing. If you're hiking solo, the empty seats at your café table on the patio have a way of filling themselves with fellow pilgrims. When abroad, Americans who would never talk to a stranger, yet alone share a table, have a tendency to gravitate toward one another. Europeans, who can be more reserved than Americans in most situations, are used to sharing tables, especially if they're from Scandinavia, Germany, or Austria where communal outdoor restaurants are more common. Similarly, sitting at the bar tells people you want to talk; sitting at your own table, especially inside, tells people you want solitude.

Nearly every village has a church, but not every village has a priest. Vocations are down in Europe, dramatically. In one of the great ironies of history, the continent that used to send missionaries to the New World now has New World priests going to Europe to minister to the dwindling number of practicing Christians. However, that's less of an issue in Italy. Pilgrim masses are rare, but you can often attend a regular mass in the morning. These are a chance to consider what has brought you to the Via, reflect on our common humanity, and imagine the faith that drove those medieval and renaissance artists and worshippers to dedicate their lives and treasure to the churches they built.

5. Eating on the Via

Italian cuisine is one of the world's favorites. If you're an American, you may not realize the variety of it since we're so used to pasta covered in a heavy tomato sauce masquerading as Italian. In Tuscany, you'll find lighter fare and a few specialties. For good reason, tourists even come to Tuscany specifically to take cooking lessons.

Breakfast

Like the rest of southern Europe, breakfast in Italy is a light affair. Bread, jam, maybe some fruit or a pastry is what you'll typically get, but if you're staying in a hotel, there will likely be some cured meats and cheeses and a selection of cereals. The hoteliers know what their guests like, so breakfast is getting larger in Italy. I'm not a coffee drinker, but of course Italians love their coffee. They don't linger over it, however, but order it to go or drink their shot of espresso standing up at the counter.

Lunch and dinner

Pilgrim menus are still uncommon on the Via, but inexpensive lunches are available from cafeteria-style restaurants and pizza sold by the slice (*pizza a taglia*).

Italian dinners come in several courses, usually beginning with an appetizer (*antipasti*) and bread. The second course is known as the *primi piati (first plate)*, and this is the pasta we think of when we think of Italian cuisine. The *secondi piati* is a meat or fish course. If you want a vegetable, this usually has to be ordered separately. Dessert is known as *dulce* and can be fruit or pastry. If you're hotel price comes with dinner, you'll be given a menu with a few options for each course.

I've dinner included in the price of self-guided trips, I wouldn't do it again only because there is so much variety to choose from. If you're in an agriturismo or in a small town with only one restaurant, you know where you're eating. But if you're somewhere with lots of choices, follow the crowd or look at menus on the wall or just let your nose lead the way. I've yet to have a bad meal in Tuscany.

I asked the proprietor of an agriturismo if Italians eat this much at every meal (I couldn't finish a third of what he served me), and he told me yes. Either the Mediterranean diet has been misrepresented in media, or the people of Tuscany don't subscribe to that diet, or they just get four to five times as much exercise as we do. The pasta course is more than enough of a meal on its own.

Buying and preparing your own food

You can buy food from shops and markets in Italy and prepare your own meal. This tends to be less expensive. Fresh fruit, bread, cheese, meat, snacks, and canned goods are easy to come by, as is pasta and rice. A picnic lunch on an Italian hillside is a special experience, and if you bring a little extra you can always invite a passing pilgrim to join you and make a new friend.

Many hostels have simple kitchens with simple cooking utensils. You can prepare your own dinner. I suggest making friends, and you can cook for them one night, and they can cook one of their national dishes another.

Well-known ingredients in Tuscany

Tuscany's dulce vita is closely tied to the agriculture of the area. The olive oil comes from the groves you walk past, the wine comes from the vineyards you walk through. The pasta is fresh and the olive oil is many times more flavorful than what's available in most US grocery stores. Other common ingredients from the region include truffles (in season during the fall), wild boar (tastes more like beef than pork), pecorino cheese (from the local sheep), and local beef (Chianina beef, to be precise, more common near Florence). Tuscan bread is traditionally made without salt, the only such bread in Italy made without it.

As in most of Europe, wine is labeled by where it's from rather than the grape. Several of the towns on or within a short bus ride (or even walking distance) of the Via in Tuscany produce word famous wine, including San Gimignano, Montalcino, and Montepulciano.

Gelato, like I said, is serious business. Gelato is made out of milk, not cream, which means it has a lower fat content (not so low that it's any healthier). Because fat coats the taste buds, the lower fat content of gelato means the flavor is more intense relative to ice cream. It is also lighter and melts a little faster. It comes in dozens of flavors in every conceivable color and is often made on the premises. A good way to tell if the gelato was made in-house is to see if the containers it is served from are metal (usually means made in-house) or plastic (usually means not). In Piazza della Cisterna in San Gimignano is a gelato shop that won the world gelato competition a few years back. I've never had bad gelato from anywhere.

Optimizing your dining experience

Anywhere there's more than one restaurant, browse. See what others are eating before you decide where to eat. Look for restaurants away from the main square, where the food may be better, more local, and less expensive. Look for places where the locals are eating, where the menu is small, and where it's in Italian. The tourism industry in Tuscany is so extensive that it's difficult to find a restaurant where the menu isn't in English, but places that only have a menu in Italian probably serve local people local food.

When you do eat out, remember that the European dining experience is slow. It's a time to socialize, unwind, and enjoy the sensory experience of eating. Eat like Europeans do, and because slow service is good service, expect to wait, and when you're ready to go, you'll have to ask for the bill. Also, in Italy tips for the wait staff are built into the cost of the meal, so you only need to leave a euro or two on the table. I typically round up, so if my meal is €8,50 and I pay with a €10 note, I leave the change on the table.

You will probably be surprised to learn that being a waiter in Italy is a career, not a job, and they get paid a living wage, in contrast to the U.S. where being a waiter is what you do until you can find career and where waiters would be homeless without tips. For that tiny bit extra you pay for your meal, you get a professional who provides great service, and very often I've had a small appetizer or drink served to me gratis

An agriturismo is a working farm that lets rooms. The use of the term 'agriturismo' is regulated to prevent hotels with a garden from marketing themselves as farms, and the result is when you stay in an agriturismo or just get a meal from one, the food is as fresh as it can be. I once had a three-course dinner in which everything but the flour in the bread came from within eyesight of the table: oil from the trees in the back yard, vegetables from the garden, wine from the vines on the next hill, wild board from the forest on another hill. If you can, splurging on a night in an agriturismo is worth it.

6. Sleeping on the Via

You have options on the Via as to where you sleep, but unlike the Camino de Santiago, there are fewer pilgrim-only options. Furthermore, because Tuscany is crawling with tourists, demand for beds is high and accommodations can be expensive. *Can be*, not *always are*.

Hostels

Pilgrim hostels are the traditional accommodation for pilgrims. Most often in churches, seminaries, monasteries and convents, these accommodations are inexpensive and often free. If it is free and you can afford it, just offer a donation of 5 to 10 euros or so. Of course, in addition to pilgrim hostels, there are also standard tourist hostels that offer more amenities at a slightly higher price point.

Because there are comparatively few pilgrims on the Via, many hostels are not open every day or staffed all day when they are open. It's a good idea to call ahead two or three days before you expect to arrive to check availability, make a reservation, and let them know when you'll arrive. I'm hesitant to say calling ahead is mandatory to ensure a bed in a hostel, but ... let's just say you'll never regret doing it. It's a hostel reservation, not a hotel reservation, so if your plans change, it's not like you're out a fee.

To stay in a pilgrim hostel, you will need your credential. Modeled on the *credentiale* of the Camino de Santiago, this is a passport of sorts that proves you're a pilgrim, granting you access to pilgrim hostels and discounts on public transportation in Tuscany. At the end of your pilgrimage, the credential serves as proof you actually did the pilgrimage.

The innkeeper will stamp your credential and direct you to your room or dormitory, which can have one bed to several dozen. Privacy and hot water can be at a premium.

Inside the dormitories, be courteous, and that means being quiet. People are napping during the day, and they're tired at night. The dorm is not a place to hang out. Do what you need to in there and then leave. This is especially important if you're starting your Via farther down the trail; you arrive fresh and ready to go and spend your first night up with friends having a communal meal and laughing it up, but the people who've already been on the Via for weeks are tired and want to go to bed. Everything echoes in these old buildings. Please don't be one of "those" pilgrims.

You will share the dorms with people who snore, and yes, people do fart in their sleep. You do too in all likelihood. It's just something you have to deal with; it does no good to wake up a snorer or to confront them in the morning. Wear your earplugs if it bothers you. What's more annoying than snoring? Listening to people complain about snoring, that's what.

Hostels all have some sort of laundry facility, even if it's just a sink outside. The clotheslines can get full, and while you can make some room for your things, it's not very pilgrim-like to just put someone's things on the ground.

There are communal spaces in hostels, including lobbies, kitchens, and patios. These are good places to read, talk with friends, and spend your afternoons. The kitchens often have basic appliances, pots and pans, and utensils, and sometimes you'll find something left behind by another pilgrim. Cooking is a good opportunity to get to know your fellow pilgrims. I find that wherever I am, sharing a meal with someone is very human, an aspect only accentuated by strange faces around a table in a strange land.

Some hostels ask you to leave your shoes and trekking poles at the door, and some don't. Some have coin-operated washing machines, and some don't. Some will do your laundry for a couple euros. Some have communal dinners and breakfasts. Some have coin-operated massage chairs. Some rent private rooms. The point is that hostels come in all shapes and sizes, and there's nothing wrong with checking the alternatives before choosing one, including asking to see the rooms and facilities. That said, much of the Via is about simplifying your life, if only for a short time. You will get more than your money's worth in a hostel.

Hotels

Because the Via is still relatively untrekked by pilgrims, the pilgrim-only infrastructure is sparse compared to, for instance, the Camino de Santiago. Conversely, because Tuscany draws so many tourists, hotels are one of the main industries. You will encounter far more hotels than hostels. They vary in price from 30 Euros to over 100 Euros. If you can find a friend, or brought one with you, a double room is usually 50 euros or less per person in a modest hotel.

There is nothing wrong with staying in a hotel. Throughout its history, people on the Via have stayed in whatever accommodations they could afford and chose to stay in. However you walk the Via is your pilgrim experience.

Hotels on the Via usually offer a breakfast, and sometimes they will offer to include dinner in the price, if not at the hotel than at a nearby restaurant. Hotels sometimes offer a laundry service, but you can wash your clothes in the bathroom as well.

Agriturismi

An Agriturismo are working farms that rent rooms. Typically, in Tuscany these are farm houses attached to a vineyard, olive grove, or both. They serve dinner and breakfast, and some offer cooking lessons, and a very few will let you help in the field or at least give you a tour of it.

While these can be expensive, they can also be worth the price. Many offer pools, the food is excellent, and the wine often came from right outside the door.

Camping on the Via

Italians enjoy camping, and you can find camping sites along the Via nearly every day. If you do decide to camp out, you'll need a larger pack, a tent, tarp or bivy, a ground cloth, and a sleeping pad and bag. Your local outfitter will be able to help you purchase those items, but you could also skip a few of them for a more Spartan camping experience.

Remember that the area around the Via may be empty in places, but that doesn't mean it's not owned by someone. Don't assume you are on public land (you're most likely not, even if it looks like it; it's probably a farm), and *never, ever start a fire*. It gets very dry in Tuscany; even if you find a fire ring, don't use. One errant spark, and you're part of an international news story about family farms getting burned down – yeesh! You are a stranger in their land, you could be a trespasser or inadvertent arsonist too, and those aren't very polite things to be. Ask permission to camp if you see someone who looks like he owns the land; you might get told no, but you might also get invited to dinner. As with all outdoor activities, leave no trace.

7. Health and Safety on the Via

The next two chapters deal with physical preparation for the Via as well as what medicines to take and what a first aid kit should contain. Before I get to that, here are some of the more common health and safety concerns about the Via.

The Via is safe, yet as with any physical undertaking, there are risks. Few pilgrims will encounter life-threatening dangers, but they do happen, and everyone should know about the signs and symptoms, both for their own good and so they can be of service to other pilgrims.

Emergencies

God forbid you should experience an emergency while in Italy or on the Via, but the risk does exist. Fortunately, wherever you are, including on the Via in Tuscany, you are never far from a town or farm

As safe as the Via is, people die on trails like the Via every year, either by being struck by cars or by over-exerting themselves and succumbing to heart failure, or exposure. Be aware of your surroundings, and be physically and medically prepared. You should talk to your doctor before you go to ensure you are healthy enough for the preparation as well as the journey.

The emergency number in Italy (and most of Europe) is 112. Here are a few words you may need, but hopefully never will:

- Ambulance = *Ambulanza*
- Police = *Polizia*
- Fire = *Vigili del fuoco*
- Doctor = *Dottore*

Blister treatment

Blisters are probably the most common ailment on the Via, and there's really no predicting who will get them. If you follow my footwear and sock advice, you'll be less likely to suffer through them, but even I get them. If you do get them, knowing how to treat them is crucial. You should talk to your doctor about how to recognize and treat a blister before you go.

Blisters form because of friction against the skin. They start off as "hotspots" that feel just like they sound, an area on your foot that feels almost like a very minor burn. The friction is damaging the first few layers of skin, and the body responds by filling the area with fluid, pushing those layers of skin out and creating the blister.

First, if you feel a hot spot, stop walking and treat it. The only excuse not to stop immediately is that doing so would be dangerous. Otherwise, stop. You are much less likely to get a blister if you treat the hot spot immediately – it takes very little time or distance for a hot spot to become a blister.

To treat a hot spot, examine it, your shoe, and your sock, and ask yourself if it's as simple as adjusting something to decrease friction. It's probably not that simple. Next, if your socks are damp, change them. Wetness makes friction worse. Then cover the hot spot with something specifically meant to cover a blister, like the products mentioned below.

The unfortunate fact is that the treatment for a hot spot and for a blister is the same: cover it, stay off of it, and wait. On the Via, of course, you can't stay off it, so all you can do is cover it and hope it doesn't turn into a blister, and if it does turn into a blister, still keep it covered. There's nothing more you can do for a blister than what you should already be doing for a hotspot, with the exception of applying antibiotic ointment to it before covering it.

My preferred blister treatment is Molefoam. It's a thicker version of Moleskin, which is a smooth fabric with a strong adhesive backing. The smoothness of the fabric helps reduce friction, and the strong adhesive keeps the bandage in place and from becoming another source of friction. The thinner Moleskin is especially useful for the small and curvy areas of your foot because it's more flexible, but I prefer the thicker Molefoam. For me, it does a better job dispersing the friction and acts as a cushion. Try both during your practice hikes if need be. I carry one package of Molefoam with me on my hiking trips, and one sheet of Moleskin (three or four sheets come in a package). That knife you brought, or the scissors in your first aid kit, can cut a piece just the right size.

When I do get a blister, I'm always sure to use antibiotic cream on it after showering and whenever I cover it. I check it when I stop during the day to see how it's holding up, I keep it as clean as possible, and I change the cover as needed.

Another treatment is called Compeed. This is a piece of waterproof, thick, flexible plastic with a very powerful adhesive. It works just like Moleskin, but it's meant to stay on until the blister heals, including in the shower. I tried this once without success (it turned into a gooey mess when it got wet, which then turned into glue when dry), but many people swear by Compeed. Whatever product you buy, read and follow the instructions on the package.

Here's what not to do to a blister: pop or pierce it. Blisters can become infected, and they are more likely to become infected if they are open. Think of your skin as a bacteria-resistant barrier, because that's what it is. The fluid that accumulates in the blister is actually helping you, and it will eventually be reabsorbed by your body.

Sometimes blisters pop themselves, or more likely depending on where it is on your foot, you'll step on it, and it will just pop (and you'll feel it, and it will be kinda gross, but not typically painful). Just keep it clean and covered, apply antibiotic ointment when you cover it and after you shower, and keep on keeping on.

How do you know if your blister is infected? If the blister or the area around it starts to feel hot to the touch, is discolored, or is abnormally painful, it might be infected. If it does rupture, the fluid that comes out should be clear and odorless; it it's colored or smells bad, it's almost certainly infected. If that happens, find a pharmacy or doctor.

So, to review how to treat a blister:

- Cover the blister with a product specifically meant to cover a blister
- Follow the directions on the blister product you are using
- Use antibiotic cream
- Change the blister cover at least twice a day – once before starting out for the day, once after showering, and anytime the cover wears out, gets wet, or peels off.
- DO NOT POP, PIERCE, OR DRAIN A BLISTER!
- Look out for infection – heat, discoloration, severe pain; milky, opaque, or odiferous drainage – and see a medical professional if you see these signs

Dehydration

Dehydration is probably the second most common ailment on the Via. It shouldn't be a problem on the Via – water is plentiful. The trick is carrying enough. There are plenty of opportunities to refill, either at fountains or at bars.

There is a saying that says if you are thirsty, it's too late and you're already dehydrated. That is flatly untrue. Is being hungry a sign of starvation? Of course not! Thirst is your body's way of telling you to drink something. It is not a sign that you are already dehydrated, but a sign that you should hydrate.

There is no magic formula for how much water you need to drink. Err on the side of caution and carry more than you believe you'll need (on any trail, in any weather, always). You'll get a feel for how much water you need during your practice hikes. I carry three to four liters based on distance, weather, and how I'm feeling

The signs of dehydration include extreme thirst; concentrated (dark) urine; dry skin, lips, and mouth; headache; dizziness; and lightheadedness. The signs of extreme dehydration include a worsening of the above symptoms; rapid pulse and respiration; shriveled, inelastic skin; and confusion. Someone suffering from dehydration should drink water or a sports drink and get out of the sun until symptoms subside. Someone suffering from severe dehydration should seek emergency medical care.

Sunburn, heatstroke, hypothermia

In terms of exposure to the elements, sunburn is the most common threat, but heatstroke and hypothermia are possibilities as well. I strongly suggest reading up on these conditions, their symptoms, and how to prevent them in authoritative medical sources, and perhaps discuss these with your doctor when you see her to talk about whether you are healthy enough for the Via.

Sunburn is a risk on the Via as with any outdoor activity. If you are particularly susceptible to sunburn, you should consider wearing long pants and sleeves. Everyone hiking in the warm months, even on a cloudy day, should apply sunscreen and reapply it throughout the day. In the cold months, consider sunscreen because prolonged exposure can result in sunburn even on a cold day.

Heatstroke (hyperthermia, or sometimes called sunstroke) is also a possibility. On hot days with much exertion, getting overheated is possible and potentially dangerous. Everyone walking the Via in the summer is at risk of heatstroke. Preventing heatstroke requires staying hydrated, trying to avoid sunburn, keeping the sun off your head, and staying out of the heat if it's just too hot. Wear a wide brim hat or a hat with a flap that covers your neck and ears. Rest when needed, preferably in the shade or indoors if the weather is hot. On hot days, rise early and try to complete your day's walk before noon. Heatstroke becomes more likely the more you exert yourself − there's nothing wrong with taking a rest day.

Symptoms of heatstroke include an elevated body temperature, altered mental state, nausea, vomiting, flushed skin, rapid pulse and respiration, and headache.

Anyone experiencing these symptoms should cease exertion and get out of the sun, preferably into an air-conditioned vehicle or building. Anyone exhibiting severe symptoms – body temperature over 103 degrees, altered mental state, no sweating or urination, increased pulse and respiration – should seek emergency medical care immediately.

Hypothermia, a low body temperature, is a possibility in cold and even just chilly weather, even in the fall or spring. It is, however, unlikely for most pilgrims unless they are making their pilgrimage in the winter, but you can get hypothermia any time you are cold, wet, and especially when you are both cold and wet, no matter the time of year, meaning the risk of hypothermia is elevated in the spring and fall, and it's even possible in the summer. Wet clothing, even if it is only wet from sweat, saps heat from your body. During the cold months and at higher elevations, it is important to know the weather before setting out. Check the forecast, and ask locals and heed their advice.

The key to preventing hypothermia is to dress in layers and stay dry. Signs of hypothermia include shivering, lips and skin turning blue, dizziness, hunger, nausea, increased pulse and respiration, trouble speaking, confusion, fatigue, and lack of coordination. As hypothermia worsens, shivering ceases, and physical coordination and confusion get worse. People exhibiting signs of hypothermia should get warm and dry as quickly as possible. Those showing severe signs of hypothermia should seek emergency medical care immediately.

Crime on the Via

Crime does occur on the Via, but it's rare and usually just involves petty theft. The Via is safe, much more so than many American cities.

Locals respect the Via, and they understand the importance of the Via to their local economies. I feel safer on the Via alone than I do walking with friends in some of the neighborhoods in my own city.

Perhaps because of the heavy tourist presence, there is also a heavy police presence in the towns along the Via. There also more pickpockets, so wear your money belt.

Getting lost

Getting lost is fairly common, but staying lost takes effort. It's easy to miss a way marker, but they are so frequent that it's difficult to go far without realizing that you've missed it. Of course, it is easier to get lost in the dark and the fog. Rarely will you have to backtrack too far to find the spot where you lost the trail.

If you really and truly lose the trail, use your judgment and either backtrack or wait for someone to come along. Perhaps your smartphone can tell you where you are. If you are somewhere where there is a risk of falling or getting hit by a car and you don't have any visibility, stop walking until you can see.

Since my first pilgrimage, it's become easier and less expensive to use smartphones abroad, and there are apps and GPS files available for each stage of the Via. I highly recommend these. They make it even harder to get lost. More on this in the **Electronics** section of this book.

Stray dogs

Dogs are common in Tuscany, but so are fences. You'll get barked at a lot by dogs fenced in behind signs reading *Atente al cane!* I've only come across one dog not behind a fence, and it was probably the only one who didn't bark at me. After about a hundred barking dogs, I mostly was ready to shout back.

If you do encounter a stray or otherwise aggressive dog not behind a fence, try to go around it or scare it off by shouting and tossing a rock or stick. If it won't budge, back up without turning your back on it and take a wide way around.

Traffic

The Via runs along, over, and across roads and interstates, some remote and others in towns. Much of every day on the Tuscan Via involves road walking, and parts of the Via are on regional highways with not so much as a guardrail between you and traffic. These sections are *not* the exception.

On these sections, walk on the left side of the road (against traffic) so that you can see oncoming cars, make eye contact with drivers, and react. Take your headphones out when walking on or near roads so you can hear traffic coming, look both ways when crossing a street, and be careful! Most drivers are courteous and make way, but the hilly terrain and winding roads mean there a lot a of blind spots, and Italians drive fast.

Part III

Preparing for the Via

8. Physically preparing for the Via.

Walking is hard. If you're like most people, you don't think it is, because you never walk very far, but walking is hard, and walking very far is very hard. You will discover muscles and tendons you didn't know about before, usually because they're causing you pain, and if you thought standing on your feet all day was tough, wait until you walk on them all day long. If you doubt it, consider that walking applies at about 1.5 times your body weight of force to your feet. Those thin layers of skin, fat, muscle, tendon, and bone that are the soles of your feet are supporting your entire body, your pack weight, plus 50%. For a person weighing in at 150 pounds and carrying a 30-pound pack, that's 270 pounds of force applied with each step. Now, depending on your stride, one mile could consist of anywhere from 1800 to 2800 steps. For me, a mile is about 2200 steps, which makes a 10-mile day – a modest day – 22,000 steps. Imagine someone hitting the soles of your feet with 270 pounds of force 22,000 times. The first 10,000 probably won't hurt, but it's downhill from there. And quickly.

I probably shouldn't have told you that because the unfortunate fact is that foot pain doesn't really go away. I've talked to long-distance hikers who have taken on considerably more challenging hikes than the Via, and everyone agrees that your feet will hurt. This chapter is more about minimizing all the other discomforts of the Via. If at the end of the day all that hurts are your feet, you're having a great day!

First, talk to your doctor. Are you healthy enough for the Via, and for that matter, are you healthy enough to get healthy enough for the Via? After traffic accidents, most fatalities on the long hikes are caused by heart attacks suffered by people who were not physically healthy enough for the rigors of the trail. I'm not a doctor or any kind of health care professional, so please talk to your doctor and take my advice for what it is – lay advice that you follow at your own hazard.

Second, consider your infirmities in general. Are you overweight? Do you have bad knees, hips, ankles, or a bad back? Are you in good shape, or even phenomenal shape? Anything you can do to get in better shape will help you on the Via, and help you period.

Everyone needs to prepare for the Via. Walking for 15 miles with something on your back is not a normal daily activity for anyone other than park rangers. Preparing needn't be burdensome, though. At a minimum, you just need to load up your pack with everything that you're taking with you and start walking as often as you can. However, that's the minimum, and it doesn't necessarily reflect the best situation for everyone.

Let's assume you're in good shape. You're physically fit, and your body is sound. In your case, you need to prepare yourself for the rigors of the Via, namely making use of the muscles you don't normally make use of, getting used to the weight of a pack, letting the skin on the soles of your feet toughen up. That can be accomplished just by adding some hiking, with a loaded pack, to your routine. Shoot for ten miles a week at a minimum, a decent Saturday hike.

Let's say you're not in good shape. Let's say you are largely inactive. Can you still do the Via? Yes, but it will be slower and harder, and your preparation needs to focus on getting your body accustomed to physical stress. Your preparation is about minimizing discomfort down the road - getting your shoulders and neck used to the strain of a pack, getting your ankles and knees and hips used to constant movement, building up muscular endurance in your legs, increasing your lung capacity, strengthening your lower back, making your heart more efficient. All of these areas will be under strain they are not used to on the Via.

So here are my recommendations on physically preparing for the Via:

- Consult your physician
- Start preparing early, and ease your way into your routine. Let your body tell you what it is ready to do. Exercise should be uncomfortable, but never painful

- Develop a well-rounded workout routine. If you do it right, you actually don't have a choice but to develop a well-rounded routine

The importance of balancing your routine cannot be overstressed. Here's a little refresher on how your body works with regards to physical activity and exercise:

- Your muscles need oxygen to work. Oxygen is inhaled through the lungs and stored in your blood, which your heart delivers throughout your body
- When your muscles are working harder, they need more oxygen
- To provide that oxygen, you start breathing harder to take in more oxygen, and your heart beats faster to deliver that oxygen to your muscles faster
- That system yields an obvious corollary: the more efficient any one of those systems (muscles, heart, lungs) works, the more efficient all the other systems will work, too. Make your muscles work better, they'll demand less oxygen, and the less your lungs will need to breath faster and the less your heart will need to pump faster. Make your heart stronger, and it will deliver more oxygen to your muscles with less heavy breathing. Make your lungs stronger, and they will take in oxygen more easily.

So yes, you should lift weights and do cardiovascular exercise. I have a weight lifting and cardio routine that works for me regardless of whether I'm preparing for a hike. Design your own routine, or ask for help from your doctor, a personal trainer, or the people who work at your gym.

There is a common misperception that weight lifting results in a lot of added muscle mass, and that's not accurate. You can lift weights and build strength and endurance without building mass. You will be carrying a fairly heavy pack, and you want your neck, shoulders, lower back, hips, thighs, and calves to be used to the weight and to how long you will be carrying it. You can read more about different types of weight lifting, but the short answer is that to build strength and endurance, you need lots of repetitions and weights of medium heaviness. If you're interested, read up on the subject, and if you're not already a weight lifter, I recommend speaking to your doctor and getting in touch with a personal trainer to help you design a workout.

Get out and hike. My training hikes are typically on Sundays so that I have enough time to get in some good miles. It's important to hike with the gear you'll have on the Via for two reasons. First, you want to test your gear. Things you take for granted may not work: are your socks comfortable? How about your underwear? Would it be helpful to have anything else with you? Is there anything you can get rid of? Are you loading your pack efficiently? Do you know how to best adjust your pack?

Second, you want to be used to carrying all this gear. I actually do my practice hikes with all manner of junk I don't need. Tent, sleeping pad, stove, fuel canister, extra clothes — anything to add weight. With water, my pack typically adds up to 45 pounds, at least 50% more than I take on any trip that doesn't involve sleeping outside. Start out hiking with the gear you are taking, and then for your last few practice hikes, carry the kitchen sink. When you step on to the Via a week later, it will feel easier, if not easy, by comparison. This is actually common sense. Think of it this way: an Olympic wrestling match is six minutes long, but the athletes prepare for it by practicing 4 hours a day or more.

Hike on varied terrain. You want to hike on flat ground *and* hills. The Via is of course a mix of both, hills lasting for extended stretches. You want to not only prepare yourself for all types of terrain, but observe how your body handles it. How hard are you breathing going uphill? How much do your quads burn? How much do your feet hurt? How fast are you going? This last one is important. If you know how fast you are, you'll be better able to plan ahead.

You want to hike at least one very long hike while preparing. You still want to pace yourself and avoid injury, but you need to build up to hiking longer distances. My first training hike when I was preparing for my first pilgrimage was 12 miles, the last 3 of which were agonizing. It was too much for a first hike, but afterwards I was averaging 15-mile days, and they weren't so bad. My longest was an overnight trip that ended up being 36 miles over about 30 hours, and it was excruciating (it also the day I learned my boots were a half-size too small for long distance hiking). But my longest day on the Via ended up being a little over 20 miles, and while it hurt and I was exhausted at the end of it, it wasn't agonizing.

Lastly, part of the point of practice hikes is to reveal your weaknesses at home where you can deal with them rather than on the Via, where dealing with them will be much more difficult. Are blisters a problem for you? Try different remedies, including different socks, wearing one sock versus two, Moleskin, Molefoam (my favorite), Compeed, Bodyglide or any other remedy you want to try. Problem with a joint? Maybe you can strengthen that joint through a specialized exercise or support that joint with a brace. Talk to a doctor or physical therapist about it. In retrospect, I'm thrilled that I got blisters on my practice hikes. It toughens the skin as they heal, and I figured out how best to prevent and treat blisters for me.

Prepare for the weather. If you're going in the summer, make sure you spend some time outside. It's hard enough hiking in 95-degree weather if you're used to it, so make sure you arrive used to it. (Sorry to anyone who doesn't live where it gets that hot).

Spend some time in the sun. I'm not suggesting that you set out to get a tan, but if you step out onto the Via officer-worker-pale, you'll end up with sunburn for sure. Use strong sunscreen whenever you spend time outside, and reapply it throughout the day.

Don't let the prospect of rain keep you from a practice hike. It might rain on the Via, after all. Think of it as a good way to check your rain gear. I recently did nine miles in a state park on a very humid June day, and I was so happy when it started raining – it cooled everything off, including me, and cut the humidity out of the air. I didn't even bother with a rain jacket.

Don't let the prospect of heat keep you from a practice hike, BUT ADJUST YOUR HIKE. I live in St. Louis, an area that produces as high a heat index as anywhere in the country. I'm not going to make myself miserable, and endanger my health, to get in a practice hike. I will, however, go out early in the day, take more water than I think I'll need, and cut my hike short with the goal of being back before noon. Same goes for hiking in cold conditions (yes, you still need a lot of water when it's cold out). If it is hot, or cold, to the point of dangerous, then I will skip a practice hike.

It's important to take at least one day of rest per week from your workout routine. When you exercise, you are basically damaging tissue, especially in the case of resistance training. You are damaging tissue, and your body rebuilds it stronger than it was before. That's how people build muscle, and note that it's actually not the burning sensation that is damaging the muscle either. It's the act itself — the lactic acid buildup is a metabolic byproduct. But your body cannot rebuild itself instantly. It needs time. If you damage the same muscles repeatedly without giving them time to repair, you will never gain any strength. It takes about 48 hours to rebuild muscle, so when you design your routine, you need to give each muscle group 48 hours between exercises to be repaired. Hence the importance of taking a rest day.

If you are in reasonable shape and start preparing for your trip 12 weeks out, you should be ready by the time you hit the Via. If you need to get in shape, start preparing earlier.

9. Shopping and packing for the Via

This chapter is really the impetus for this book. The more I learned about hiking by actually doing it, the more I came to look askance at so many books that attempt to tell novice hikers what they needed on a walk like the Via. Some of them got the basics right but lacked detail. Others didn't give advice so much as instructions, which is the author's way of saying that their way is the only right way. Others just gave bad advice. My objective here is to give you options and knowledge so that you can make your own informed decisions.

Packing for the Via is not that different from packing for any trip: you'll need a piece of luggage, shoes, clothing, medicine, paperwork, and a few other items. The difference is in the type and functionality of what you need. It's really nothing to be intimidated by.

On a note of trail etiquette, it's considered rude to discuss the merits of another person's gear with that person, and it's considered by many more to be a boring topic of conversation when on the trail, except when seeking specific advice. Off trail, most people love to talk gear and give advice.

To get one thing out of the way, there is this ridiculous rule of thumb that says a hiker should carry no more than 10% of their body weight. I have a hard time picturing whoever came up with this "rule" doing an extended overnight trip with no resupply. I don't say that to suggest that you should carry more than 10% of your body weight, but to point out that someone hiking the Pacific Crest Trail (2,663 miles from Mexico to Canada) is hiking on much harder terrain than the Via, is carrying a good deal more than 10% of their body weight, and is doing it for six months as opposed to the Via's two, carrying food, tent, sleeping gear, and water treatment for a week or more without resupply. These people are not superheroes – they're just like you and me.

I don't want to downplay the importance of minimizing the amount of unnecessary weight you carry on the Via, but I do want to point out that there is a difference between minimizing and obsessing. Some people are into ultralite hiking, and the obsession is part of the hobby for them; it's fun to them to find ways to save a quarter ounce. But a lot of people obsess about their pack weight because they think they have to, and in my opinion, these people on the whole cause themselves way too much stress about it. My philosophy for packing for any hike is to decide what I need, then to decide what I *really* need, then to decide if there are lighter weight alternatives or modifications.

Where to shop

No, this book isn't sponsored by anyone, and I'm not getting paid by any outfitter or retail outlet (but if wishing made it so...). Store and brand recommendations are entirely candid.

Recreational Equipment, Inc. (REI) is the main outdoor equipment retailer in the U.S. They have a knowledgeable staff and excellent selection. They are also a co–op that you can join for a one–time $20 lifetime membership fee (as of this writing), and you'll get 10% back on eligible purchases (which is almost anything you pay regular price on; you get the money back in the form of a dividend, in store credit or cash, in the Spring). That will add up to quite a bit by the time you're done outfitting yourself for the Via. They also have a no–questions–asked return policy, which is especially advantageous as you're trying out gear on your practice hikes. Don't take advantage of the policy, but use it appropriately as needed. Returned items end up in periodic garage sales at REI stores, and these are good opportunities to get quality gear at low prices. Members also get access to coupons and other benefits non-members do not. Clearance sales at the change of seasons or right after the new year (a lot of outdoor gear gets updated each year, like a car model year, so the old stuff goes on clearance) offer good discounts.

Amazon carries everything, including packs and boots. Packs and boots/shoes should be tried on in a store, but then you can buy them on Amazon if you need to or just want to. However, I don't find that Amazon is much, if at all cheaper when it comes to quality gear, and returns can be a hassle, especially if you find yourself needing to return gear that just didn't work out. For the small miscellaneous items you'll need, Amazon is a good bet.

Don't forget your local outfitters and retailers, too. Their staff tend to be very knowledgeable and can give you lots of advice on places for practice hikes in your area. But if you do go to a retailer, local or national, don't spend a bunch of time pumping the staff for advice and then not buy anything from them. That's just not right. A lot of these people are on commission, and the time they spend with looky-loos is time they could have spent with a paying customer.

Via –specific items

The first thing you need is a *credenzale*. This is the document that proves that you are a pilgrim. Without it, you can't stay at pilgrim-only accommodations. To prove to the basilica authorities in Rome that you have earned your *testimonium* (the certificate attesting to your accomplishment), you need to get your credenzale stamped at least once a day, and after reaching Viterbo (110km from Rome), it's advisable to get it stamped at least twice a day. It sounds like a hassle, but it's actually convenient and a joy. It's easiest to get it stamped at hotels and other accommodations. Some churches have a stamp, and in some towns, you go to the city hall or tourist office, which can have hours not very helpful to pilgrims. It's best to get it stamped when you arrive in the afternoon rather than trying to do it in the morning when you leave when places may not be open yet. Some bars also stamp, and as you get closer to Rome, they become more common. The document becomes a narrative of your journey. Mine are my most prized possessions.

You can wait until you get to your starting point to get your credenzale, or you can arrange to have one sent to you by https://www.viefrancigene.org/en/. Other resources provide them as well, and if you're taking a guided or self-guided tour, your tour company will most likely take care send you one or have it waiting for you at your first hotel.

You will need a daily Via guidebook. The gold standard for English–speaking pilgrims is the Lightfoot Guide series by Paul Chinn and Babette Gallard. These guides are published in volumes that break the Via into three long stages, and, within these, into daily stages. The books list common stage breakdowns, distances, elevation changes, accommodations, and towns. You'll use this guidebook to plan your stages. If you're hiking just a section, only take the pages with you that you'll need. Bind them in something to keep them together, even just masking tape. I recommend something that will stand up to getting wet since you'll probably carry your guidebook pages on your (sweaty) person.

I strongly recommend a guidebook for Europe and/or Italy (or whatever country you'll be spending most of your time in). Rick Steves' overview of European travel, *Europe Through the Backdoor*, and his country- and city-specific guidebooks are best sellers for a reason: his books are thorough, up to date, and insightful. They contain information on travel to and from Europe, travel within Europe, money in Europe, traveling with electronics, documents to take, and much, much more. I keep an electronic copy of his Italy guidebook on my smartphone while on the Via and have stayed in hotels he has recommended. Rick Steves' travel company also makes money belts (see below) and a cover for binding loose guidebook pages. His website contains a lot of general information about traveling in Europe, and you can purchase a few key travel items directly from his site.

Footwear

There are a couple of old myths about hiking footwear that seem to get repeated from generation to generation. The first is that you need heavy, stiff hiking boots with good "ankle support." The second is that you need to break in your boots thoroughly.

YOU DO NOT NEED HEAVY, STIFF HIKING BOOTS! You are not going mountaineering. You are not carrying heavy loads. Hiking *shoes* are a fine option for the Via. I've heard of people doing just fine in regular athletic shoes, though I wouldn't advise it because of the rougher areas. Hiking sandals are gaining popularity for warm weather hiking, but bear in mind that sandals don't always fit as well as shoes, and that you'll spend a lot of time picking pebbles out of your sandals.

This is surprisingly not obvious to a lot of people, but boots that are soft and comfortable don't need to be broken in. Do your gym shoes need to be broken in? The technology overlap between hiking shoes and other kinds of shoes is at the point where most boots don't need more extra care than an everyday shoe. What's more, shoes that fit well when you buy them generally don't need to be broken in, even stiff leather dress shoes.

So what should you look for in hiking footwear? First, you want a shoe with a good tread. Does it look like it will grip a wet or slick surface, like a gravelly hillside? Vibram soles are now very common on hiking footwear. If you see their name on the shoe, it's a safe bet that they have a good sole. But not seeing their name doesn't mean it's not a good sole. Use your judgment. How deep and aggressive is the tread?

Second, is the shoe waterproof? Water will get in through the tops and around the edges of the tongue if you submerge your foot, but it's nice being able to walk through a couple inches of water, or even just some wet grass, without getting your feet wet. I mostly prefer to buy boots that have a Gore–Tex (or an equivalent) lining between the inner and outer layers of the shoe's upper. Gore–Tex is a thin membrane that breathes, allowing moisture to evaporate, but doesn't allow water in. Most shoemakers also have their own version of Gore–Tex that they call by another name, and they work just as well. Sometimes with Gore–Tex, if your boot gets very wet, you'll notice that your foot feels wet but actually isn't.

A lot of people detest waterproof hiking boots and shoes because they feel these are not breathable enough, leading to sweatier feet that negate the waterproofing and make you more blister-prone. I believe this is a personal preference. I'm kinda/sorta starting to feel this way, though.

Are they breathable? Most shoes breathe, including leather boots. Some shoes even have mesh side panels. The exception is if they have a waterproof membrane that isn't Gore–Tex or a similar product, or if they've been finished with certain kinds of water proofer or polish. On this last point, go with your gut– does it look like air is going to pass through there? If it's shiny, it won't (and these shoes are going to get messed up – why would you want shiny hiking boots?).

Does the shoe have a rand? The rand is the strip of material that covers the front of the toe. On most boots, it's part of the sole (or at least appears to be) and is made of the same material. This material protects your toes (and you shoes) from all the things you can stub your toes on.

Size AND Width. Your feet swell when you walk. In fact, they can swell up to two shoe sizes larger than normal. So, when you buy a hiking boot, buy one full size up AND one full width up. Bear in mind that you might be the kind of hiker that prefers two pairs of socks.

A "wide" shoe width corresponds to an EE width in most brands. Pay attention to the letters, not whether the salesman or website says it's wide. Keep in mind that the dimensions of size and width are not the same across brands, or even across shoes made by the same brand.

When you go to buy your boots, go in the afternoon when your feet will be slightly larger than first thing in the morning (because they've been under you all day). In the store, try on the boots with the socks you'll most likely be wearing.

Here's how to try on hiking boots:

1) Lace them up and walk around the store. Does your heel slip? Does the toe box or heel feel tight? Does the arch feel too high or too low? Does the shoe feel too tight or way too loose? Does anything rub uncomfortably? Yes – put them back. These shoes

will cause you pain and give you blisters. No – proceed to step two.

2) Most outdoor stores have a short wooden ramp you can walk down to see if your toes will hit the front of the boot when going downhill (which results in lost toenails after a while). Yes – try a half size larger. No – move to step three.

3) On the carpet, stomp your feet in a forward motion, like you're coming to a very sudden halt. Do your toes hit the front? Yes, and it hurts. Put these back. Yes, but it doesn't hurt. These could be the shoes for you. No – either these are too large or they're laced too tightly. Your toes should hit the front if you really stomp, but they shouldn't be smashed into the front. The stomp test is kind of a crapshoot, but it's a good indicator.

These tests aren't foolproof. It's ultimately a judgment call: does this shoe feel like it will be comfortable after 15 miles? It's hard to tell because most shoes feel good when they're brand new, so think very hard before you decide. The corollary to not needing to break in your modern hiking boots is that modern hiking boots don't break in. If it's not comfortable in the store, it will NEVER be comfortable on the trail. And never let a salesman tell you otherwise. If they do, they don't know what they're talking about and/or just want to make a sale, and your feet are your best friends and worst enemies on the Via. Treat them kindly.

Expect to spend $100-$250 on your footwear depending on type, quality, and brand. I'm of the opinion that you get what you pay for when it comes to hiking footwear.

Backpacks

Everyone has bought shoes before: the product if not the particulars are familiar. Not so with backpacks. A sporting goods store could carry dozens of different backpacks, and this choice is just as consequential as buying boots.

These backpacks are not what you took your stuff to school in. They are heavier, they are adjustable in a bunch of different ways, and they come in sizes. So when you go to the store for the first time, ask to be fitted for a backpack. The process is simple. They have a plastic sheet with some markings on it (they're inches/centimeters) and a nylon belt. Put the belt around your waist with the plastic sheet in the back. The salesman will check to make sure that the middle of the belt is situated on your Iliac Crest (the tops of your hip bones), which is where the middle of your pack's waistbelt should sit, and then he'll press the sheet to where your neck, shoulders, and back meet (typically where most people have a small convex curve of the spine). Taking note of the marking, he'll tell you whether you're a small, medium, or large. Then you unbuckle the sheet from your waist and stop feeling ridiculous.

Some packs don't come in small, medium, or large, though. They come in small/medium or medium/large instead. The salesperson can tell you which to get.

What if you're on the rotund side? Sometimes the length of the pack for you will be a medium, but the medium comes with a smaller belt size than will fit you. Then get the large. A larger size may ride high on your shoulders, but the belt is the main load–bearing part of the pack – you can't skip it.

Some packs are unisex, some are made specifically for women, and some are made specifically for men. It's usually the case that if a pack is made for women, there's a corresponding male or unisex model.

Women's packs usually have hipbelts more suited to a woman's hip structure, a slightly different profile more conforming to the shape of a woman's back, and the sizes may correspond to different measurements (just like a woman's medium T-shirt is smaller than a man's medium). For this reason, women's packs are usually a few liters smaller than the corresponding male or unisex model. This is also true within the same model line, with a small-size pack having a few liters less room than the medium, and the medium slightly less than the large.

Because every part of a pack is adjustable, the unisex models really are unisex for people with the most common body shapes and sizes. Some industry professionals question whether packs need to designated as being made for women or men at all.

Backpacks have frames. It used to be that every pack was made on an external (you could see it) aluminum frame. Now most packs have an internal fame (it's built into the backpack), and it's made of aluminum or carbon fiber. Carbon fiber weighs less than aluminum but costs more. External-frame packs cost less than internal, but they are heavier, bulkier, and less comfortable. The last time I saw one on a trail was when I crossed paths with a young army officer out for a hike with his Army-issued pack on, and the needs behind that design don't apply to the Via.

There are also frameless packs. Some of these have a back sheet that gives structure to the pack, and these are as good as packs with a frame, though they mostly fall into the ultralite category and won't carry a lot of gear comfortably. Some frameless packs have no structure at all, which saves some weight but leaves all the weight that's there on you, not the pack.

I prefer a frame because the purpose of the frame, in addition to providing a structure to the pack, is to take weight off of your shoulders. The weight of the pack is held by the frame, the frame is held up by the belt, the belt held up by your hips – your center of gravity and strength.

Backpacks have a lot of pockets. A pack should have 5 to 7 pockets, including the main compartment, but that's not to say that one with more or fewer is a bad pack. The main compartment is just that – it holds most of your stuff.

The top of the pack is a pocket. It's a handy place to keep things you want easily accessible like keys, important papers, a little spare cash, your pocket knife, your lunch, etc. Sometimes these are detachable and form a fanny pack – a nice feature I've never had occasion to use.

There should be a pocket on either side above the hipbelt. These fit a water bottle, but note that even if you can get a bottle out of one of those pockets with the pack still on your back, depending on the pack and your reach you may not be able to get it back in without taking your pack off. If that matters to you, try doing it in the store.

There is usually an outside pocket, called a shovel pocket, which covers the main compartment and usually has no zipper but does have a buckle. It's handy for storing things you want easily accessible. A rain jacket, or some TP (or if you're camping, a trowel for digging catholes).

On either wing of your hipbelt should be a zippered pocket. They're not large but hold things you might want quickly. I keep a cell phone in one, sometimes a protein bar, sometimes a pocketknife, and usually a washcloth for mopping my brow and cleaning my hands.

Your pack might also have a separate compartment for your sleeping bag. This is especially common on larger packs, and while nice for organization and accessibility, it is not strictly necessary. I've yet to come across a pack that did not have a zipper at the bottom so that separate compartment or not, it's easy to get your sleeping bag out without having to disturb everything else in your pack.

A nice feature on one of my packs is a waterproof map pocket on the underside of the top pocket. It's a convenient place to keep not just maps but your important papers, especially on an international trip.

Most packs open from the top (top-loading packs), but some open from the front (front-loading). It's purely a preference.

Others features you should look for are hydration sleeves and ventilation. Hydration sleeves are dedicated spaces to slip a hydration bladder (see below). On some packs, this sleeve is on the outside of the pack, between the main compartment and the back panel (the part of the pack that rests on your back). On others, this sleeve is inside the main compartment and is really just a nylon pouch for separating the bladder from your stuff, with a small hole in the side of the pack to feed the drinking tube through. I strongly prefer the former setup as a full hydration bladder is a large and unwieldy thing. There's a reason no one sells bags of water — it's a pain trying to stuff one inside your backpack when it's full of your other stuff. Also, if the bladder does leak, I don't trust the internal nylon sleeves to keep anything dry.

Ventilation refers to the way the back panel of the pack is built. There are three kinds. The first type is a standard back panel and doesn't have a special name: it just sits directly on your back and is often made of soft, padded nylon. I strongly advise against this type. It doesn't really qualify as ventilation because by sitting directly on the back, and being made of a material that doesn't breathe, it doesn't ventilate anything. The only advantage to packs with this type of ventilation is that they are less expensive.

The second type of ventilation is a mesh back panel. This is sewn to the pack and is made of mesh with some foam in key spots underneath to aid support and create air pockets between your back and the back panel. Your back closes off most of the airflow, but your back is not pressed directly against the bag, so some air is moving.

The third type of ventilation is the *suspended* mesh back panel. On this type of backpack, the frame is more curved (while still molding to the shape of your back) to create more space between the back panel and the bag itself. Mesh is stretched over the frame, so air is moving between your back and the backpack.

Here's a front and profile view of a pack with a standard back panel:

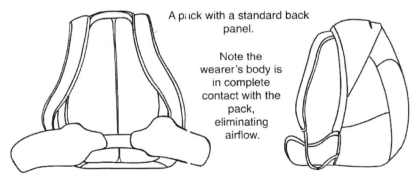

A pack with a standard back panel.

Note the wearer's body is in complete contact with the pack, eliminating airflow.

Here's a front and profile view of a pack with a mesh back panel:

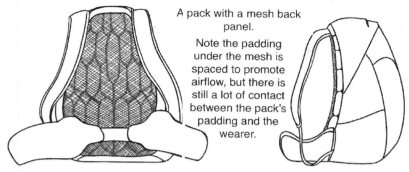

A pack with a mesh back panel.

Note the padding under the mesh is spaced to promote airflow, but there is still a lot of contact between the pack's padding and the wearer.

Here's a front and profile view of a pack with a suspended mesh back panel:

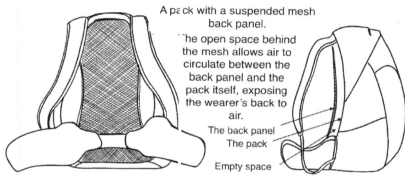

A pack with a suspended mesh back panel.

The open space behind the mesh allows air to circulate between the back panel and the pack itself, exposing the wearer's back to air.

The back panel

The pack

Empty space

The suspended mesh back panel gives a lot of airflow, but there is a tradeoff: I have yet to find a backpack with both an external hydration sleeve and a suspended mesh back panel. I suspect this is because the hydration bladder would bulge into the space between the mesh and the bag, canceling out any airflow. I prefer the non–suspended mesh back panel with the external hydration sleeve. I enjoy the airflow of a suspended panel, but realistically, every part of you, including your back, is going to sweat when you hike no matter how much airflow there is. For me, the convenience of the external hydration sleeve cancels out the slight increase in comfort I get from a suspended panel.

How big of a pack do you need? Some people say you should buy everything you're going to take with you and then decide how big a pack you need. I say that this approach leads you to taking more stuff than you need. Buying the pack first puts a hard limit on how much stuff you can take: only what fits in the pack.

For my first pilgrimage, I bought an Osprey Talon 44. The "44," or any number that follows a pack make and model, is the volume of the bag in liters. Sometimes you'll see pack volumes in cubic inches, which is actually kind of a pain (2200 cubic inches versus 2600 – how is anyone supposed to intuitively know how much bigger that is?). I think 44 liters is the perfect size for an unsupported Via, but not necessarily the perfect pack (bad news: the perfect pack doesn't exist).

Packs themselves weigh a few pounds, anywhere from one pound for a small bag to six or seven pounds for a large one. The more features, the heavier the pack. Packs in the ultralite class have fewer features and weigh less. You don't need many features, right? And the less weight the better, right? Maybe.

The component of a pack that's easiest to save weight on is the padding in the shoulder straps and hipbelt. Because padding helps to distribute the weight of the pack, having less padding means that the pack will put more pressure on your shoulders and hips. This means that the amount of padding determines how much weight a pack can hold *comfortably*.

My Talon 44 is meant to hold 25 to 40 pounds, but beyond about 30 it's not very comfortable. I have a larger pack, an Osprey Aether 70, that's meant to hold 50 to 65 pounds. The Talon weights 2 pounds, 6 ounces. The Aether weighs 5 pounds, 3 ounces. I prefer the Aether for any hike where I'm carrying more than 30 pounds – it weighs more, but I don't feel the weight as much because the pack is doing more of the work by distributing the weight better. If only they made the Aether or something like it in a smaller size... (hint, hint, good people at Osprey).

Everyone has to figure out the right combination of size, weight and feature set for them. For the Via and similar trails, unsupported, I believe the right size is somewhere between 35 and 50 liters (probably more like 38-48), and my preference is for packs somewhere in between ultralite and every feature available.

If you are going on a supported pilgrimage and will not be carrying all of your belongings every day, a daypack should be sufficient. You'll need to decide what should go in your daypack, but at a minimum it should include water, a first aid kit, rain gear, a change of socks, anything important or valuable you brought with you, and it still should have room left over for lunch and a change of clothes. A pack this size will typically run from 10 to 25 liters. My own pack for these purposes is 22 liters, but 18 would do fine.

When you go to buy your pack, try it on in the store, and ask the salesman to put some sandbags in it so you can feel the weight. Be suspicious: every pack feels fine with 25 pounds in it when you just put it on. Will it really still feel good after 15 miles? Put some sandbags in a backpack and then wear it while doing the rest of your shopping in the store to get a sense of how the pack feels after a half hour, but you still need to make a judgment call about how it will feel after six or eight hours of hiking.

Backpacks are adjustable in several ways to provide a close fit that puts the weight of the pack in the right places. Before you put on a backpack for the first time, loosen the straps on the hipbelt, the shoulder straps, the sternum strap, and the load lifter straps.

To adjust a pack:
- First, after loosening those straps, put it on.
- With your pack on your back, start by buckling the hipbelt and tightening it so that it hugs, but doesn't compress, your hips.
- Then tighten the shoulder straps as much as you comfortably can; it helps to shrug your shoulders while bending forward to lift the pack up, then tighten the straps by pulling down and back quickly before the pack settles back down. Having done this, the middle of the

hipbelt should still rest on the tops of your hip bones (the Iliac Crest). If they don't, the shoulder straps are too tight or too loose, the harness needs to be adjusted (see below), or the pack is the wrong size for you.

- Buckle the sternum strap. the purpose of the sternum strap is to keep the shoulder straps from sliding off as you walk; it doesn't need to be tight, and it should go across your sternum, not across or under your nipples.
- Lastly, snug down the load lifter straps (above and behind the shoulder straps), which pull the top of the pack closer to the tops of your shoulders so that the top of the pack doesn't sway from side to side or pull you backward as you hike.
- As a last step, you can very slightly loosen your shoulder straps so that the weight of the pack comes to rest more on the hipbelt.

Once you have the load lifter straps adjusted correctly, they should not need to be adjusted much in the future except when you're putting more weight or volume in your pack than you normally do. All the other straps need to be loosened when you take the pack off and tightened when you put it back on every time.

Remember that packs are sized by the length of your torso, but these reflect a range of lengths. Most packs these days, other than true daypacks, have adjustable torso harnesses to make the length perfect. It varies by pack, but the shoulder harness on adjustable packs is often secured to the back panel or the material behind the back panel with Velcro, and in this way it becomes an extension of the back panel. By adjusting the harness, the torso length of the pack can be made longer and shorter (within a range, of course – this is not a substitute for the right pack size).

Here's how to use an adjustable torso feature:
- If your shoulder straps are not resting on your shoulders when the hipbelt is on your Iliac Crest, or if the shoulder

straps only rest on your shoulders when the hipbelt is below your Crest, your pack is too long for you, and you need to shorten the torso length or return the pack for a smaller one.

- If the hipbelt is positioned above your Iliac Crest, is on your Crest but isn't bearing much weight, or only bears weight when you loosen the shoulder straps so much that the pack hangs away from your back, then the torso length is too short for you, and you'll need to extend the torso length or return the pack for a larger one.

You'll most likely have to try the pack on several times to adjust the torso to the right position for you, but your salesperson can be a great help in making the first adjustments in the store. It helps to have weight in the pack when finding the right adjustment. One this is adjusted perfectly, you can leave it alone pretty much for as long as you have the pack. I like to adjust mine so that the very top of the back panel rests at the very top of my scapulae. Unfortunately, adjustable harnesses are not, so far, available on packs under about 20 liters.

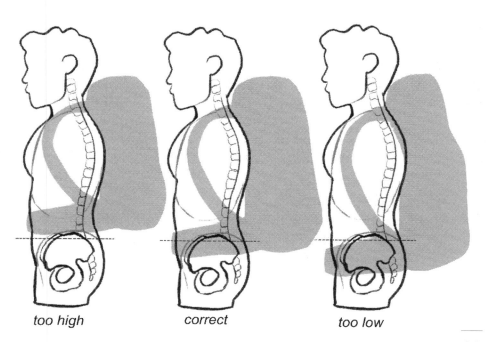

too high   *correct*   *too low*

You can find many online videos showing how to fit, adjust, and pack a backpack, including several very good ones on the REI website. Most pack manufacturers also have instructional videos on their websites.

There is also an art to packing a backpack. The goal is to distribute the weight in such a way that the pack and your core – not your shoulders – are doing the work. It's all about putting stuff in the right place, and it's easy:

- The sleeping bag goes at the bottom.
- To provide some additional structure to my bag, I like to put my sandals, vertically with the soles facing out, at the bottom on either side of the sleeping bag.
- The heaviest items in the pack should go in the middle of your back. The Via doesn't require anything very heavy, so it's a good place to put your second set of clothes or your cold weather gear (if you have any).
- Above that, you can stash your toiletries and towel. They're the first things you're going to want when you get to your accommodation.
- I keep my rain cover and rain jacket in the shovel pocket, which makes them easy to grab in a hurry.
- The top pocket contains things I need regularly or might need while on the trail and don't want to have to root around in the main compartment of the bag for: first aid kit, lunch, things like that.
- The hipbelt pockets can serve a similar role as the top pocket.
- Lastly, if I have anything I just don't need on the trail itself (like electronics for the plane ride), I stuff it all the way at the bottom, out of my way.

Finally, a word on brands. The most widely available in the U.S. are Osprey, Gregory, Deuter, and REI, and they're all good. Each brand tends to have some design elements common across their models, but these are mostly aesthetic or structural more than functional. I have a penchant for Osprey packs, but that's probably just because they made the first pack I ever bought, and I stuck with what's familiar.

Expect to pay $150 to $300 for a pack. Less means heavier and/or fewer features, more means lighter and/or more features. I believe in buying the best pack you can afford because it will determine how comfortable, or not, you are on the trail second only to your footwear.

Socks

Socks matter just as much as shoes. Every hiker has their own preferred sock strategy. Here are your basic options:
- One thin sock. Keeps your feet cool and feels more natural.
- One thick sock. Adds some cushioning.
- One thin sock (typically a liner sock) under one thick sock. More cushioning, and the liner sock wicks moisture away from your foot and into the thick, outer sock. Some find that the inner and outer socks slide over one another so that the friction is between them and not between your foot and the sock.

The bottom line is all three strategies are meant to prevent blisters, and the only way to figure out which one works for you is trial and error. And like most everything else for a long-distance hike, hiking socks are not like regular socks.

Hiking socks are expensive. There's no getting around it. Figure on spending around $10 to $15 per pair and on donating some that don't work for you. It's a bummer, but socks are one of those places where you just can't skimp on hiking gear.

Never wear cotton socks while hiking. They absorb moisture rather than wick it away, and that means blisters. And while they seem soft at home, they lose their softness when air–dried (and they take longer to air dry). You want wool socks or socks in a technical fabric.

Wool is a great insulator. It wicks moisture. It's soft. And regardless of what you might remember from childhood holiday sweaters, it doesn't itch. Some wool hiking socks are even the very soft Merino wool. Wool socks come in a variety of thicknesses, but most of them are thicker than technical fabrics.

Technical fabrics are designed to have a lot of the same properties as wool. Most liner socks are technical: polypropylene and polyester mostly (though some liners come in silk). Technical fabrics do retain odor more than natural fibers, but who's ever heard of a rosy smelling sock anyway? Besides, you'll wash your clothes daily.

SmartWool is a company that makes performance clothing, including socks. Their wool socks are a treated Merino wool, and they also sell some in technical fabris. If you're going with a wool sock, I recommend this brand or a similar technology (other manufacturers treat their Merino socks, too, and use a different trademark name).

My socks are my secret weapon. When I first started hiking, I tried the two–sock method, a polypropylene liner sock under a SmartWool sock. I got blisters. I tried changing my socks mid–day, and I got blisters. I tried just one sock, and I got blisters. They were concentrated on the balls of my feet where my toes start. I came to the conclusion that the friction from the sock, and not from the boot or ground, was causing my blisters.

I have a thick foot, and it forms a gap between the sole and the toes where my socks can work their way in and move around, causing friction and blisters. I looked into some goofy remedies before finding Injinji socks – these are socks made for runners, and they have *individual toes*. They're made from treated Merino wool (called NuWool by Injinji), and they are skin–tight. By being skin tight, they fill in the space between my toes and soles without moving around, causing no friction and no more blisters on the balls of my feet. The only drawbacks are that they're don't provide much cushioning (though they do come in different thicknesses), and they take some practice to put on. But they are my favorite piece of hiking gear (and they lead to fun conversations when people see my individually socked toes).

Bottom line is socks are trial and error. Your practice hikes will be key in helping you select the right sock for you. Avoid cotton socks, and find the right fabric, thickness and number of socks for you.

Water

Water is plentiful along the Via. The water in Western Europe is perfectly potable for Americans – you will not become ill from the tap water. You can even drink from public fountains (the spigot, not the pool) so long as it doesn't have a sign saying you can't, and you can buy bottled water anywhere you stop for about a euro or two. The bottles you buy are just like the reusable bottles in the U.S., so you can refill them and reuse them.

I prefer to carry reusable water bottles. I drink a lot of water, two to four liters a day even when I'm not hiking, so I like carrying all my water, and I like it to be accessible. The side pockets on your pack will fit a 1–liter Nalgene bottle (Nalgene is a brand name, but it's become synonymous with all plastic water bottles of that size and shape). If you're going to carry nothing else, carry a 1–Liter Nalgene bottle.

But as I said earlier, the side pockets are not always easily accessible when your pack is on your back. Assuming you can twist your arm backward to reach the bottle and get it out, you may not be able to get it back in without taking your pack off. And one liter is not as much water as you think it is. What if, like me, you need to carry three liters? Then you'd need three bottles and three places to put them.

That's where hydration bladders (also called hydration reservoirs) come in. A hydration bladder is a durable plastic bag for holding water with a long, flexible rubber tube for drinking out of. At the end of the tube is a bite valve – when you bite down on it (gently) and suck, water comes out; when you're not biting down on it, it's sealed and doesn't leak.

On any hydration bladder, the drinking tube (not the urethra, I've been corrected and assured) just comes out the top of your pack or through a port in your pack, loops over your shoulder, and secures under some elastic bands on the shoulder strap (if you have them). Water when you want it without having to take off your pack or stop walking, and the weight of the water – the heaviest single item you will carry – is positioned in the middle of your back, where your heaviest items should be, rather than on your sides.

Camelbaks are the original hydration bladder, and they work fine. But their bladder is just a plastic bag with a tube. Whether the hydration sleeve on your pack is internal or external, with a full pack there's not a lot of open room to shove a bag o' water. How easy do you think it is to get a bag of water into a narrow space that's being impinged upon by the stuff in your pack, keeping in mind that the bladder needs to maintain its shape well enough so that the flow isn't blocked? It's a royal pain, especially at 6am when you're trying to walk out the door.

Enter Osprey, the same company that makes all the packs I own. They make a hydration bladder that has a wonderful addition: a stiff but flexible plastic backing. This gives structure to the bladder and makes it easy to get it in and out of a hydration sleeve. For my money, I think their bite valve is better than Camelback's, too. These features add a fraction more weight, but they save a lot of hassle. Another nice feature is that the Osprey bladders have a loop at the top, and their packs have a small buckle in the hydration sleeve – buckle the bladder in through the loop, and it won't slide down to the bottom of your hydration sleeve, taking the tube with it, as you walk.

Osprey also added a magnet to their drinking tube that connects to a magnet on their sternum straps, so the tube doesn't flop around loose with every step.

I carry a 2– or 3–liter Osprey bladder as well as a Nalgene bottle on the trail. When I stop, I drink out of the bottle to avoid draining the bladder. I want that full when I'm walking and can't want to take off the pack to get a drink.

No one likes a bladder infection, in this case mildew or mold. It's absolutely true that a hydration bladder is more difficult to fill (marginally) and to clean (definitely) than a bottle. A Nalgene bottle can be put in the dishwasher, a hydration bladder cannot. You probably won't clean your hydration bladder while on the Via beyond just a rinse (probably also true of a Nalgene bottle and definitely or a disposable bottle), and that's sufficient. When you're home, though, and between practice hikes, you need to clean it – damp and dark breeds mold, even though hydration bladders contain anti–mold materials. You can buy kits and special tablets to clean hydration bladders. I recommend the kits – they come with a brush that lets you get inside the bladder; a longer, flexible brush, like a pipe cleaner, to get into the tube; and a special hanger that holds the bladder open to airdry. Just follow the instructions and let the bladder hang long enough to dry out. You may need to hang it upside down from a clothes hanger to make sure it drains completely. However you clean it, just don't put it away wet.

Trekking poles

Almost every pilgrim has a walking staff or trekking poles. Why use a staff or trekking poles? For safety and support. Poles and staffs transfer some of your weight from your legs, and especially knees, to your upper body while allowing you to keep at least two points of contact with the ground at all times. Is there a thigh–high rock in front of you? Plant your poles up there first and pull yourself up. Are you on a steep downhill? Use the poles to slow yourself down. Is the ground uneven or slippery? Having more points of contact makes it less likely you'll fall, and my poles have saved me from what would have been numerous bad falls.

I appreciate the emotional pull of a wooden walking stick – the wood just feels appropriate, like something a medieval pilgrim carried. And with some extra hassle, you can mail one back to your home as a souvenir that will mean more and last longer than anything else you might buy along the way. That said, I don't recommend them. Not because they don't do a decent job but because modern trekking poles and staffs do a better job.

A trekking staff is a modern walking stick, while trekking poles come in pairs like ski poles. They're made of aluminum (less expensive) or carbon fiber (lighter weight). The handles are neoprene or cork. They have a metal or rubber tip (usually interchangeable: use the rubber ones for less clacking noise and less scratching up the rocks on the trail – leave no trace). They are adjustable to fit your height. I prefer poles because one of them is always on the ground, whereas the staff gets picked up with each step. And yes, you do develop an emotional connection to your trekking poles just like you do a walking stick.

I've seen a lot of hikers incorrectly using their trekking poles. All trekking poles have a wrist strap. Your hand comes in from *underneath*, not from above, so that the strap goes across your palm. This transfers your weight to the pole via the strap so that you don't have to white–knuckle the poles to put your weight on them. Sometimes it helps to palm the poles, putting your hands on top of the handles to place more weight on them. This is especially helpful going downhill.

I will sometimes take my hand out of the straps on my poles on very rough or slippery sections or trail and grip the handles extra hard. This is because if I do take a fall, I want to be able to let the poles go rather than have my poles, and wrist, potentially go one way and my body another.

You can't carry trekking poles, staffs, or walking sticks on an airplane. They have to go in checked baggage.

Sleeping bags

This item comes in low on my gear priority list, but I'll give it a thorough overview anyhow.

Sleeping bags come in temperature ratings. These ratings are the air temperature in which the average man or woman could sleep comfortably in the bag assuming they are wearing a base layer (long underwear) and a hat. This rating is actually ten degrees colder for men than for women – European Union regulations require the rating to account for the fact that men, on average, stay comfortable at lower temperatures than women due to a higher average metabolism (this is why in the summer time the men who work in your office are comfortable and the women are wrapped in blankets – the formula for setting the temperature in an office building was developed in the 1960s, when few women worked in an office and no one cared anyway how they felt).

Some people say that this rating is actually a survival rating and the manufacturers are pulling a fast one, but for Via purposes, it's a moot point: you're most likely sleeping inside. Pilgrim dormitories can have a lot of bodies in them, boosting the temperature; they don't always have a lot of windows, and you might not always be near one (and the person who is may want it closed); rural Italy is often not air conditioned; and you're probably going during a warm month. You don't need a sleeping bag rated for sub–freezing temperatures, and you don't want one. The warmer the bag, the heavier and bigger it is.

Sleeping bags are insulated with down (yep, goose feathers, or more likely duck feathers, which are cheaper) or synthetic materials. They're both warm, but the down is warmer for the weight and bulk. In fact, down is the best insulator known to man. We have been unable to discover or invent a material superior to what nature has given waterfowl. The downside to down is that when wet it loses its insulating properties until it dries, which takes a long time. But again, it doesn't matter because you're sleeping inside. Synthetic down is less expensive, almost as light, and almost as warm.

At home, store your sleeping bag on a hanger or in a large stuff sack, never in its compression sack. This prevents the insulation from losing its loft.

For my first pilgrimage, I bought a synthetic sleeping bag with a high temperature rating, 55 degrees. I figured that would be fine, but it was actually a lot more than I needed. For all the reasons I already mentioned, it can be warm in pilgrim accommodations to the point where I have trouble sleeping. Also, every pilgrim accommodations I stayed in provided a heavy blanket plus a sheet. I don't know how often the blankets get washed, but the sheets look liked they got washed daily (they were white, at least). The sleeping bag became an extra 2 pounds in my pack.

A nice alternative is a sleeping bag liner. This is basically a sleeping bag the same thickness as a sheet and not insulated at all. It provides some warmth, you know it's clean (or at least it's your own filth), and it weighs less and takes up less space than a sleeping bag. They come in silk as well as synthetics; the former is more expensive, but takes up less room and weighs less, while the latter is less expensive and is often treated to repel insects. I don't know if that includes bedbugs, but I figure it can't hurt. Mine is synthetic.

Some people are content to just take a regular bed sheet from their home, and some take a silk sheet to save on weight and space. Ultimately, whether you take a sleeping bag, sleeping bag liner, or sheet depends on personal preference and time of year. When I go on pilgrimage now, I take a liner just in case and rarely use it.

Clothing

Don't wear blue jeans. In fact, don't wear cotton. Cotton is heavy, it absorbs moisture rather than wicking it away, and it takes a long time to dry. You'll be hand washing your clothes most nights. You don't have the time to let your jeans or favorite t–shirt dry. Besides, on the trail you will be more comfortable in technical fabrics.

Polyester technology has come a long way. It's soft, drapes well, breathes well, and dries fast. The majority of technical-fabric hiking clothes are polyester.

Underwear is one of those things that you don't spend too much time thinking about. You pick a style, and you stick with it. And then you think nothing of it going on your first practice hike – until you're halfway into it and your thighs are licorice red and so raw that your own sweat burns. Yeah, that happened to me (more than once). The best hiking underwear is a technical fabric that pulls moisture away, dries quickly, and fits snuggly.

I recommend boxer briefs. By extending down the thighs a little, they help prevent chafing there (and other bits too – yeah, that happened to me, more than once). The brand matters less than the style and fabric (quick–dry polyester), though.

The most common pants you'll see on the Via are convertible hiking pants in polyester. The lower legs zip off to form shorts. They're lightweight, they dry quickly, and they have cargo pockets if you need an extra place to hold something. The big brands for these are Columbia, Patagonia, and REI.

Many hiking pants come with a simple nylon belt with a plastic crimp buckle. If not, you can buy one cheaply. The adjustability of these belts is superior to leather and linen, both of which become stiff and difficult to adjust when wet or sweaty. It's not uncommon for a belt to loosen up as you walk, and the ability to snug a nylon belt with a crimp buckle down just a little bit is ideal.

There are a variety of good–looking outdoor shirts these days, but for actual hiking, I like a t–shirt in a technical fabric. Russell Athletic makes shirts in a material called Dri–Power (other brands have other names for this technology). It breathes well, it dries fast. They're the same shirts I wear to the gym; I own many. Nike, Champion, and all the other major active clothing brands produce similar fabrics.

In the evenings, it can feel pretty good to change into something different from what you wore all day. There are a number of brands that carry outdoor shirts that are a little nicer than a t–shirt but are still lightweight and made of quick–dry material. I like to change into one of these shirts after hiking all day.

Virtually all hiking clothing, in a technical fabric, is now made with sun protection in mind. There is typically an SPF rating prominently displayed on the tag. Still, use sunscreen, even if it's a cloudy day, and reapply often.

I don't wear bright colors at home. I'm an earth tones kind of guy. But not when I'm hiking. I wear bright shirts, my shoelaces have blaze orange in them, and my packs are silver, blue, or red. If I get hurt, if I'm ill, if I'm lost, or if I'm walking near traffic, people will be able to see me. Save the camouflage and earth tones for hunting trips. Hiking pants and shorts tend to come in shades of green and brown, though, so no help there.

You do need a hat of some sort. They make a huge difference helping you stay cool and feeling good on a hot day. Because so much of the Tuscan Via is on exposed ridge lines with no shade, you need a hat to keep the sun off your head and neck and out of your eyes. You can go with a wide brimmed hat, but you can also get a ballcap–style hat that has a flap (often detachable) that covers the back of your neck and your ears. Hats also come in breathable, lightweight fabrics that are designed to help you avoid sunburn, but this is the only piece of clothing where I don't see anything wrong with cotton, so long as it's not heavy like the expensive kind of sports team hat. Some people like straw hats because they are light and shed water. Whatever it is, it just needs to be lightweight and functional. I like the ballcap style because you can wear it under the hood of a rain jacket to keep the hood from sagging low over your eyes.

Sunglasses are also a must. Your eyes need to be protected from sun damage as well, and you'll look cool in them. Sunglasses made for athletics often have lenses that cover more of your eye, offering more protection above, below, and to the sides.

Rain gear

This is one of those items where you definitely get what you pay for. You can go inexpensive and get a plastic or rubber jacket for under $20, but after wearing it for about five minutes, you'll regret it deeply. The whole point of a rain jacket is to avoid getting wet, but by choosing a cheap, non–breathable rain jacket, all the moisture (i.e. evaporating sweat) from your body stays inside the jacket. You'll end up soaked in your own sweat (and no one will want to sit by you).

Again, breathable fabrics are best, and usually this means Gore–Tex or a similar material for a rain jacket. There are so many options here, but this is pretty straightforward. Look for a jacket that is lightweight, has a hood with a drawstring, and packs down to a small size. Some of them even pack into their own pockets. This is an item I keep in the shovel pocket of my pack so it's handy.

Two rain jacket tips: buy a larger size than you normally wear, and try it on in the store. You may need to put the jacket on over more than one layer, for instance if it's cold and raining, so the larger size keeps you from hiking through Italy looking like an overstuffed sausage. The larger size also promotes airflow.

Trying it on in the store is also a chance to cinch down the hood to see how it fits; I've found that on some jackets, my field of vision is too small when the hood is cinched, and I've always been very big on seeing where I'm going (my whole family is). A handy trick for this is to wear a ballcap under your hood, though, and then you can cinch the hood down without it impeding your vision.

You'll need a rain cover for your pack. Yes, your pack is probably made out of nylon, and nylon is water resistant, but nylon is not waterproof, and neither are zippers. Some packs have a built in rain cover that's stored in a pouch at the bottom of the pack. These are handy, and I don't understand why every pack doesn't have one. If your pack doesn't have one, you'll need to buy one. They come in sizes and have an elastic cord so you can fit it to your pack well, both to keep it watertight and to keep it from flapping around in the wind. These can be balled up pretty small and kept in your shovel pocket.

Rain pants are an option I don't take advantage of except in cold weather. I'm just not that concerned about my legs getting wet unless its chilly or cold. I feel like my jacket is enough for me, and I find the extra layer of pants to be uncomfortable for hiking. But if you don't like being wet, don't like the idea of hiking in wet pants, tend to get cold easily, or are hiking in chilly or cold months, rain pants are great. If you are hiking in potentially cold weather, then rain pants are a must. All the rules about rain jackets apply to rain pants.

If you really want to stay 100% dry (or at least close to it), you can get rain gaiters, too. Gaiters are waterproof sleeves that go over the top of your boot and around your lower leg so that water cannot get in from the top of the boot or tongue. If you're hiking in a wet area or month, these are worth it. They are reasonably priced

Should you consider a poncho? Ponchos are cheaper than rain jackets. They're open on the bottom, so by definition they are breathable. They keep most of your legs dry without rain pants. And they are big enough to cover you and your pack, so you don't need a rain cover. The downside? It's hard to use trekking poles with a poncho on, you lose a lot of range of movement for your arms, they're heavier, and while breathable, they still trap some moisture around your upper body. Some people prefer ponchos, others don't. It's purely a preference, though it can be a good budget saver, too.

Camp shoes

You most likely do not want to wear your hiking footwear all day, which works out great because many accommodations won't let you wear your muddy, smelly boots inside.

Sandals are a good "camp" shoe in warm weather because they're lighter than shoes and can offer relief from blisters and sore feet. At the end of the day, it's nice to just let your feet breath. You can take a pair that's waterproof for use as shower shoes, but a pair of non-leather sandals will do the same job and be more wearable everywhere else, too. Some people prefer Crocs: they are super–light, waterproof, and whatever you think of their appearance, they are functional.

If it's too cold for sandals, some lightweight athletic shoes or slip-ons are a good alternative. I also take one pair of comfortable, non-hiking socks for the evenings.

Cold weather gear

Whether you need it or not depends on the time of year and your preferences. You know what you need to be comfortable, so just check the average temperatures when and where you'll be going and decide. If you do need it, and November to March you definitely need it, here's my advice.

Fleece is warm and lightweight, and it breathes. Breathability is especially important in cold weather clothing because however cold it is, you're still exerting yourself, and you'll still sweat. You want that moisture to evaporate. Fleece's drawback is that's it's not windproof, but windproof materials aren't always breathable. If your cold weather gear isn't breathable, you'll end up wet and potentially even colder. So for an outer top layer, consider a fleece jacket or vest. It doesn't need to be thick: 100– or 200–weight fleece will do because...

Layers! Layers are the absolute key to staying warm in cold weather. Layering traps air between the layers, and your body warms that air, creating insulation. The thinner a layer, the closer to your body it should be to maximize this effect. If you find that you're still cold despite your fleece jacket, put your rain jacket on over it.

Long underwear is a choice, and it can be a good one if you tend to get especially cold. It comes in all manner of material, but unless you are going in the deep of winter, you want polyester, polypropylene, or silk. Silk is warmer than you'd think, transfers moisture, is extremely light, and packs small, but it's not cheap and doesn't have a long shelf life (even, or perhaps especially, the artificial varieties). Polypropylene is thicker than silk, often coming in a double layer, and is fuzzy–warm. Polyester comes in many kinds and is usually a good halfway point in warmth between silk and polypropylene.

Gloves and a hat are necessary for cold or sometimes even just chilly weather. When you're hiking, your body sends extra blood to your leg muscles. When it's cold, your body sends extra blood to your core. In other words, your hands will get cold if it's chilly out.

A wool knit cap does just fine, as does fleece, and look for a hat with an internal ear band that's windproof. As for gloves, I like mine on the thin side, and if need be I can always jam my hands in my pockets or even put socks over them.

If you're hiking in very cold temperatures, I recommend wool mittens.

An alternative to fleece is down. Down jackets are without doubt the warmest you can buy, and they pack down to a small size. If you're doing your Via in the winter months, down is probably the best choice for you, provided the shell of the jacket is breathable. Down is very warm, however, so consider if you will be too warm with a down jacket or vest given what time of year you're going.

On my most recent pilgrimage, I decided I didn't want to take a fleece jacket but still wanted something warm just in case. I ended up buy a wool long-underwear shirt two sizes too large and wore it as a comfortable, if not fashionable, sweater. It did the job and took up less room.

I'm a cautious soul who likes it on the cold side. That's part of why I choose mid- to late autumn for my trips. The weather can be cold and damp in Tuscany that time of year, and even if it's just chilly, the wind on the ridges can cut through a t-shirt easily. I've not always needed the thin cold weather gear I've brought, but I always take it. Just in case.

How many sets of clothes do you need?

Two. One to hike in, and one to not hike in. You'll be able to wash your clothes daily, and because you bought quick–drying technical fabrics, they'll be dry before you go to bed every night (and you should bring them in before dark as it can get foggy and damp many evenings).

I hike in a pair of convertible pants and a t–shirt, and I spend the evenings in a second pair of convertible pants and a button-down shirt. For sleeping, I wear a pair of gym shorts

Toiletries

This isn't camping, so you can, and are expected to, bathe and wash your clothes daily. You're may be sharing close quarters with strangers; it's only courteous that you don't stink. Whatever toiletries you use at home, bring them along. However, don't bring more than a 10–day supply. People in Europe bathe too (despite stereotypes), so you can restock in drug stores along the Via. You may not get exactly what you like to use, but you'll avoid carrying a lot of heavy toiletries that take up a lot of space. Besides, it's only for a little while.

By now everyone knows that there are limits for carrying liquids and gels onto planes: you can't have any containers that are larger than 3.4 fluid ounces, and they have to all fit in a single, quart–sized Ziploc baggie. Because I'm a frequent business traveler, I found out through trial and error that Nalgene and GoToob make the best set of travel–sized containers for storing smaller amounts of liquid toiletries. They're durable, and most importantly, the lids stay on and stay tight. They sell sets that include containers of various sizes, including squeeze bottles.

The small–sized Nalgene set has the perfect sizes for air travel, in my opinion.

Of course the restrictions on the size and number of liquids and gels you can bring onto planes do not apply if you're checking your luggage, but the travel–sized containers are still perfect for taking small amounts for hiking: carry only what you need, and the good brands won't open in your pack.

If you need a prescription medication that is in liquid, gel, or lotion form, you can pack it in your carry–on luggage in its original bottle. Bring a copy of the original prescription. Contact TSA or your airline for details.

One thing to not bring is a bar of soap. A wet bar of soap that doesn't dry out, for instance if it's in a Ziploc bag, turns into goo pretty quickly. Instead, I take some liquid body soap, also in one of my Nalgene containers.

I wear a beard, so when on the Via I just stop shaving entirely and go *au natural*. If you'd rather not, carry a disposable razor and the smallest container of shaving cream or lotion you can. I still use a shaving lotion, but if I did decide to shave while hiking, I'd probably choose shaving foam because the travel–sized cans are so small and light.

I suppose it goes without saying that a travel–sized toothpaste, toothbrush, and a small comb are what you need. You can also use a travel–sized deodorant, or just a mostly empty regular size.

You will need your own towel if you plan on staying in hostels. Regular bath towels are not ideal for the same reason that regular clothes are not ideal: they are too heavy, too big, and take too long to dry. Instead, pick up a hiking towel from your outfitter. These have a microfiber texture, are light, small, and dry very quickly. They come in different sizes up to five feet long. I carry two: one large one for bathing, and a smaller washcloth that I keep in my hipbelt pocket to mop at my brow, blow my nose, or whatever else I might need a clean(ish) cloth for.

No one talks about it on the trail, and most Via narratives don't mention it, so I don't know if other people carry toilet paper with them. It certainly makes sense to unless you want to find a novel one-time-use purpose for your extra pair of socks. You can buy travel–sized rolls of TP at the drug store, but I find that travel packages of baby wipes are better. They hold up better, and you can use them to clean your hands and face as well (getting the order of these three uses right is critical).

As the classic *Everybody Poops* points out so well, they do this in Italy, too, so don't try to carry enough TP to last your whole trip. You can buy it in Europe. It's also smart to carry a small bottle of hand sanitizer.

Regarding makeup, guidebooks and Via narratives have a lot to say. I won't say much either except that I think it's unnecessary. No pilgrim is looking their best, plus you have to carry it. But if it makes you feel good, then go for it.

Washing your clothes

If you're going on just a week–long trip, you can purchase individual packets of laundry detergent in the travel section of local drug stores. Considering that you are only washing one outfit, the amount of soap in one of these packets is actually more soap than you need, but once opened, you can't reseal them, and besides, six or seven of these packets together weigh maybe an ounce and a half. Or a longer trip, plan on buying soap in Europe. You can also use body soap or shampoo on your clothes.

There's no great secret to washing clothes by hand: fill a sink or tub with water and soap, add in your clothes, make sure everything gets wet and soapy, and then … well, it was clearer to our great–grandmothers who had washboards and those roller bar thingies they would wring clothes in. If you're fortunate, the tub you're washing in has a kind of washboard attached to it and you can vigorously rub your clothes on it. Otherwise you just kind of rub your clothes vigorously against themselves to try to dislodge dirt, and swirl them around in the water. Rinse until the water runs clear, or mostly clear anyway, wring them out as thoroughly as you can, and hang your clothes to dry on the clothesline. It leaves something to be desired relative to a modern washing machine, but when you look at your wash water, you'll see that you are indeed getting some nastiness out of your clothes.

You will need your own clothespins (at least one per item. I took one for each sock, one for my boxers, two for my pants, and two for my shirt.) Many guidebooks recommend taking a length of cord of some sort for your own personal clothesline. I did once, but there isn't always a place to hang it outside. Worst case scenario, in my mind anyway, is that over the back of a chair, or even laying out flat on the grass on a sunny day, your clothes dry easily (because you bought the technical, quick–drying fabric!). I've found hanging my clothes around the bathroom over the radiator, if I've staying in a hotel, whether it's turned on or not, doors, windowsills, and towels bars has them dry or dry enough by morning. Some pilgrim hostels and hotels have washing machines (coin operated), and some will even do your laundry for a fee.

If you are going at a time of year when the late afternoons and evenings are cold or chilly, your clothes may not dry no matter what fabric they are. Hang them outside until dark, then hang them inside, and if you're lucky you can hang them on a radiator that's actually working. You might have to put on damp clothes in the morning, but not much more damp than they'll be after hiking in them for a half hour. I've skipped washing clothes when it was chilly and I arrived too late in the day, knowing my clothes will still be very wet in the morning.

Medicine

I want to emphasize again that I am not a doctor, and I strongly recommend that you speak to your doctor about any medications you should take with you on the Via, and I even more strongly urge you to follow your doctor's instructions and recommendations. What follows is what I take on my pilgrimages, and why. Always seek and follow your doctor's advice and instructions.

For prescription medications, take all you will need in the original bottles, and ask your doctor for a copy of the prescription with the generic name in case you need a refill while you're over in Europe. For the same reason, it's a good idea to have a list of all medical conditions you have, if any.

One item you can ask your doctor about is a sleep–aid for the trip. I find it helps on the plane to knock me out for most of the flight, and it's helpful to combat jet lag, or a noisy pilgrim hostel. Be warned that some of these are very strong. For instance, Ambien can cause you to have vivid dreams, and some people have been known to behave strangely on it (including reports of Ambien users stripping nude on planes while asleep).

If you doctor does recommend or prescribe a sleep aid, consider trying out a dose at home before you leave to see how you react to it (following all the instructions from your doctor, of course). I took an Ambien for the very first time about 45 minutes prior to a flight to Spain and within ten minutes found it difficult to stand and walk in a straight line – had my flight been delayed, I'd have had a serious problem. The gate agent would not have been out of line to question whether I was inebriated. I've learned to not take anything until I reach cruising altitude.

For over–the–counter medications, I take enough to last me ten days, and this is the only item I pack preparing for the worst. The reason I recommend this is because it's just easier if you know you're probably going to need a certain OTC medication – you know what works for you, and these usually don't take up much space or weigh much.

Ibuprofen is such a hiking staple that it's picked up a nickname in hiking circles: Vitamin I. Hiking discomfort is about feet and joints and inflammation, so the anti–inflammatory properties of Vitamin I are much appreciated, as are the analgesic properties. I carry a small bottle.

Whether you're doing a bus tour or walking the Via, perhaps diarrhea is the most common ailment among travelers. Whatever remedy you use at home, consider taking some with you on the Via.

First aid kit

You need one in the hopes that you won't need one. I carry a small, one–person first aid kit supplemented with a few items.

What should a basic first aid kit contain? An assortment of Band–Aids and bandages in various sizes, a roll of medical tape, tweezers, some cotton swabs, gauze, antibiotic ointment, burn ointment, a couple doses of OTC painkillers, and some safety pins. Any one–person first aid kit bought in an outdoor store should contain these and a few other items in a handy zippered pouch. I add a few more things to mine:

- Extra safety pins. They can fix a broken zipper and they can be used to hang still–wet socks or other items on your backpack to dry
- Small scissors
- Additional antibiotic ointment. If you get a blister, the small amount in the first aid kit may soon run out
- Earplugs. I find that they don't help and actually keep me awake, but judging from Camino narratives, many people use these in pilgrim hostels to cut down on the snoring, talking, tossing, turning, and farting of their fellow pilgrims at night

- An emergency whistle. If you are injured, don't count on your cell phone working. Count on someone nearby hearing your very loud whistle
- Waterproof matches. I can't imagine an incident on the Via that requires building a fire, but better to have them and not need them
- Extra batteries for my headlamp. This is a handy place to keep them
- Small, cheap flashlight. Just in case – there is no worse feeling than being stuck in the dark in an unfamiliar
- Duct tape. You can wrap a few feet around a pencil or buy small rolls (about the size of your thumb) specifically for carrying on hikes. Whether to fix your gear or fix yourself, duct tape is a wonder tool
- Sunscreen

My first aid kit is also where I keep my blister treatment, and the top pocket of my pack is where I keep my first aid kit.

You might find in your practice hikes that your knees or ankles get especially sore. I can't count the number of time I've turned my ankles while hiking. I wear a brace on both ankles now when I hike. If you have any joint issues, speak with a knowledgeable healthcare professional about whether a device such as a brace will help you, and if so, take it with you on your Via.

Electronics

I'm sure if you asked 10 veteran pilgrims whether you should take any electronics on the Via, you'd get at least 11 opinions. Yes, I think it makes sense to carry some electronics on the Via. I don't think they're distractions, I don't think they're barriers, and I don't think they should be used in lieu of talking to other pilgrims. I do think that you're halfway around the world, you have a lot of transit time, your life doesn't stop while you're gone, and electronics, especially smartphones, tablets, and cameras, are a valuable way to enhance your trip, add some convenience, and capture your experience. And I think this is especially true if you plan to do any traditional sightseeing in Europe or in the major cities on the Via.

The electronic you definitely need is a headlamp; no one disputes this. Get yourself a good headlamp (not a flashlight) and carry an extra set of batteries. I keep my headlamp in the top pocket of my pack, but I take it out and leave it next to me on my bed at night in case I need to get up and so I can see what I'm doing as I pack up in the morning.

I take my smartphone on the Via. If you're traveling with others, a phone is especially convenient since most people hike at different paces, and you'll want to be able to coordinate with each other.

Know your cell phone contract and the charges you could face for data, texts, and calls in Europe. If you are interested in being able to use your phone on European cell networks, you need to call your cell provider to unlock the phone and add international service. Depending on your device and provider, you may need to purchase a European SIM card, which you can do in the U.S. or Europe. Buying a prepaid cell phone or SIM card in Europe is another option.

In my case, my regular phone can be used in Europe, though I pay a $10 per day charge if I use any data at all that day (so if it's turned off or on airplane mode all day, no charge). To me, it's worth that cost to have the device I keep all my information in and use for navigation.

I recommend seeking advice on this topic from your service provider and from a European travel guidebook for more information.

Beyond just being a phone, though, I use my smartphone to make my travel easier. With the Internet access, I can use it to confirm reservations, book ahead, download information, store documents, and solve problems. It's my music player and my library on planes and trains and busses, and you can even download audio guides for touring cities and sights.

I don't recommend that anybody take a cell phone and plan on talking or texting or emailing as though you were back home – you want to be present on the Via – but I also don't see a reason to not take advantage of the technology to enhance your experience and make travel easier. If you're worried about not being able to resist the temptation, just remember that it could cost a small fortune to call or text people while abroad, depending on your contract.

If you are taking your smartphone, disable data in the settings, or turn on airplane mode, unless you plan to use, and pay for, data service. Be sure you understand your contract and what you'll be charged for while traveling – it can add up very quickly. Note that some mobile providers allow you to use data for a flat rate in Europe, regardless of how much you use, but this, too, adds up quickly.

Taking my own smartphone with me and paying a flat rate to use data have made all of my foreign trips immensely easier. All of my important documents are in the cloud and accessible on my phone; I use it to look up information about places I'm going or sights I've seen or will see; it's my journal and sometimes camera; and it holds GPS files for the Via and other hikes.

GPS files typically come in a .gpx or .kmz file format. You can Google "GPS files for the Via Francigena" and get several results, each one a folder containing the GPS files for all the daily segments of the Via. These files need to be paired with a walking, hiking, biking or running app. Some of these come with a subscription fee or upfront cost, and others are free. I've found MapMyWalk to be easy to use. Between trips, I always forget how to do this and have to Google it, but you upload the GPS files to the app as routes you can save, then select the route – in this case the segment of the Via you're on – and it will show you a map with a red line marking the path and a blue dot that's you.

All smartphone-based GPS have gotten more accurate over the years, and now the map will show not just where you are but which direction you're facing. A little triangle button will center the screen on your location, and you can zoom in or out as much as you want. In the years I've been using this on my pilgrimages, I've not gotten lost once and hardly even need to think about whether to turn right or left.

Depending on the phone and app you are using, GPS may or may not use data (the latest iPhones do not, to my knowledge), so you can keep your phone in airplane mode and still use the GPS, though you will need data to select the route if it is saved to the cloud and not the device's built-in storage.

GPS is power-hungry and quickly drains a phone's battery. I've found the best solution is a battery case that charges your phone. Mine is a travel essential to me, and since I began using it, I don't think my phone's battery has ever been below 100% (the case battery is used first, then the phone's) even if I'm only charging once a day. An external battery is also a good option, and one I sometimes bring as a backup on my travels for other devices I may have with me.

Some people take a tablet with them on the Via such as an iPad or Kindle. I took my Kindle on my first pilgrimage. I used it on the plane, but not on the Via – I was too tired to read and more interested in my fellow pilgrims anyway. But a tablet is a good way to store important travel documents (see below), though smartphones do the same thing (what's an iPad but a big iPhone that doesn't make phone calls?).

Some guides suggest not taking a camera, feeling that they detract from being in the moment and build a wall of separation between you and the experience. I found that persuasive at first, but on my practice hikes I found myself occasionally taking out my phone to snap a picture. I ultimately decided that I did want to take a small point–and–shoot camera on pilgrimage, and now I have to factor the price of printing and hanging pictures into the cost of all my pilgrimages.

As with everything, I searched for a camera that was small, light, and maximized functionality. I'm a not inexperienced photographer, so I'm well aware of the quality that gets lost with a point–and–shoot, but carrying several pounds of camera gear just isn't worth it to me. I chose a Canon Powershot SX260 for its size and zoom; there's definitely better out there now, but it takes good pictures. I carry it in my pants pocket where I can get to it quickly. Remember to take extra batteries and memory cards (I take two of each).

If you're taking electronics, you'll have to take the chargers you need, and remember that you'll need a socket adaptor (European plugs are two *thin* round prongs, not to be confused with South Korea's two *thick* round prongs). European electric grids are more powerful than American ones, so read your devices' manuals to be sure they can handle the extra power; if they can't, you'll need to buy a voltage adaptor (this is NOT the same as a socket adaptor). Most electronics work on both voltages, but check yours just the same.

I take a watch. It's not necessary, but I find it handy, especially while in transit. You're probably used to using your smartphone, but bear in mind that you may not have it in your pocket all the time, and you may need to be cognizant of saving the battery.

Miscellaneous

I find these things useful to have, for obvious reasons.

I carry a small pocketknife with a straight–edged blade. Maybe you'll need to cut a string, or a piece of cheese, or a blister pad – it's just handy to have. You can pick up a Swiss Army knife if you like, and that's probably a good idea if you plan on picnicking a lot. The corkscrew will be handy if you're a wine drinker.

D–rings, also called carabiners, are useful for hanging something off of your pack. I always carry one and just leave it hanging from the carry handle on my pack.

Bandanas are useful as just a piece of cloth. Get it wet and wrap it around your neck to stay cool, use it to clean your hands, or as a mini picnic mat.

I take a medium–sized but light nylon bag to use as travel bag on the plane ride over and on trains and busses. I stuff it in the bottom of my pack while I'm on the Via. At night in a dormitory, I place my phone, camera, wallet, and money belt in this bag and put it at my feet.

Should you take powerbars or other food? Perhaps a treat you really enjoy if it's small and lightweight. I'll own up to taking a few protein bars with me, but only because I like having something handy to eat on the go and know they never upset my stomach.

Items to help you organize

Some hikers don't like them, but I do: stuff sacks. The argument the folks who don't like stuff sacks make is that instead of a pack filled and full, you end up with a pack full of smaller bags, lumpy and difficult to distribute the weight. I think they exaggerate the former, I disagree about the latter, and I prioritize the convenience of having stuff sacks to organize my life on the Via or any trail.

A stuff sack is just a nylon bag with a drawstring and a toggle to cinch it closed. They come in different sizes. Here's what I use:

- 1 medium sack to hold my second set of clothes
- 1 medium sack to hold my toiletries, including my towel (the extra room is helpful for taking your valuables with you to the shower)
- 1 small sack for holding electronic accessories
- 1 small sack for my underwear, socks, and sleeping shorts
- 1 small mesh sack for holding my laundry supplies

Compression sacks are stuff sacks with straps that can be tightened to squeeze out all the air and save space in your pack. If you're taking a sleeping bag, you definitely want a compression sack to make it easy to fit in your pack and o it doesn't take up too much space. In its compression sack, my 55–degree sleeping bag is about 6 inches long by 4 inches deep by 6 inches across, compared to a lot more volume when it's not compressed. I also use a compression sack to store my cold weather clothing. I figure these are the bulkiest items of clothing I'm carrying and the least likely I'll need, so who cares if they're a wrinkled wad?

The top pocket of your pack and the shovel pocket are sufficiently small that you don't need to worry about organizing those areas. Just focus on the main compartment, think about what will be in there, and how (and where) you're likely to use it.

A money belt is a pocket on an elastic strap that buckles around your waist under your pants to foil pickpockets. Wear your money belt: keep your large bills, credit cards, passport, driver's license, insurance cards and travel tickets in your money belt, with smaller bills in your pocket or a wallet.

An alternative, which I like, is the hidden pocket. It's the pouch part of the money belt, but instead of an elastic strap, it has two belt loops. You thread your belt through it and then flip it over your waistband into your pants so it rests on your thigh. It's harder to access than a money belt, but I find it more comfortable when hiking.

Whether it's a money belt or a hidden pocket, if you can find one in a water-resistant or waterproof fabric, it will help keep the contents dry.

Speaking of wallets, get a cheap nylon wallet for the Via – a leather wallet will absorb sweat and get pretty funky (I learned this by sweating halfway through mine on a July day). My wallet is where I keep that day's spending money (because you just get a lot odd looks for reaching into your pants and coming up with a €50 – go figure).

You can keep your other important documents in a Ziploc baggie in your travel bag.

Documents

This is absolutely an area where I strongly recommend looking at a European travel guidebook for advice. Here's what I take:

- My passport. But you do not need a visa in Western Europe
- Some other photo ID. Your driver's license is fine, and it's necessary if you will be renting a car in Europe. You need this in case you lose your passport
- Health insurance card
- Traveler's health insurance card. See below about travel insurance
- Transportation tickets (the originals plus a copy)
- Hotel reservations (the originals plus a copy)
- A list of contacts I might need and that somebody else might need. This should have your insurance information on it and phone numbers to contact your credit card companies, bank, and cell phone provider, the local embassy, your doctor(s), and your emergency contacts (with their title in the relevant language). This is also a good piece of paper to write down all your prescriptions and medical conditions.

You're probably printing out copies of your own tickets and reservations, so two copies should be sufficient. You can keep one copy in your money belt and one copy in your travel bag at the bottom of your pack. I use electronic boarding passes and documents while traveling in the U.S., but I prefer paper while abroad – don't count on the airports you are going through to have that technology in place, or for it to be working if it is.

You will also need a photocopy of your passport and driver's license in case you lose either one. It's not a bad idea to memorize your passport number, driver's license number, and all your credit card information (including the pins) for just in case.

Do you need travelers' health insurance? It's cheap (often less than $20). Best case scenario you won't need any healthcare on your trip; worst case you do, and you're covered. Yes, Europe has a great socialized medical system, and yes, many doctors on the Via will treat a pilgrim for free (according to rumor), but won't you feel better knowing that you're covered for the price of a modest dinner? Note, though, that most travelers' health insurance policies don't cover injuries sustained during certain activities, including hiking (or trekking, as they typically call it). What they define as trekking – the Via is not a wilderness hike – isn't clear, so call and ask. You may be able to get a special policy or supplement. Note also that your regular policy may cover certain kinds of care in Europe – read your policy or call your insurance company to find out.

Your smart devices are also useful for storing documents. Save an electronic copy on your smartphone or to the cloud (it's usually the same thing now) and tablet if you have one AND email a copy to yourself. It will live in the cloud, accessible wherever there is Internet access. It's also a good idea to email a copy to your primary contact back home, along with your flight numbers and itinerary.

Adding it up

That's all you need. Easy, right? Just to help you out, I've included my packing list in the appendix.

When done, it can add up to $500 to over $1,000. I've laid out the reasoning for every piece of gear, feature, and fabric, but like I said, however you do your Via is a great way. Get the gear you can afford from anywhere you can find it. But never cut corners on items meant to keep you safe.

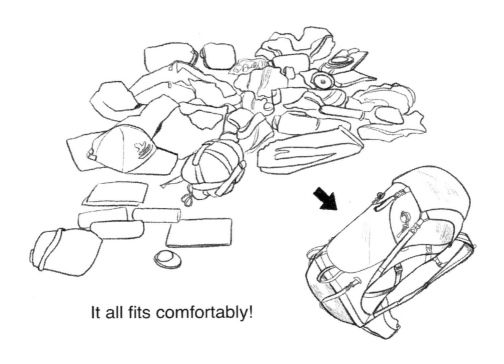

It all fits comfortably!

What you don't need to take

Here are some things you don't need:

- A tent (unless you plan on sleeping outside)
- A sleeping pad (unless you plan on sleeping outside)
- A camping stove and fuel (no need to cook outdoors, and can't take the fuel on an airplane)
- A month's worth of anything, except prescription medications. You can buy what you need in Italy.
- "Nice" clothes or shoes. At least not on the trail. If you plan on doing some sightseeing that would include more than hiking apparel, you can mail it to yourself at your hotel or the post office wherever your destination is.

10. Conclusion

A pilgrimage is a mobile meditation, a chance to reflect on the course of our lives and our development as human beings. It matters little whether one embarks on pilgrimage for the adventure or for spiritual progress: there is no avoiding the changes that pilgrimage brings. Pilgrimage simplifies our lives, divests us of our belongings, breaks us down and builds us up again with new confidence. We are who we are on pilgrimage; all of our weaknesses and strengths are revealed and tested. And by going so far from our everyday lives, we temporarily shed the many roles that we play, the roles we use to protect ourselves from the world, the roles that keep us from having to be honest with ourselves and each other. Far from being escapist, pilgrimage is where we are most real.

When you return, you'll find that you remember every detail of your journey. You'll think about your Via almost daily. You will test the patience of your friends and family as you talk and talk about the Via. But the hardest part of the return is holding on to the lessons you learned, the breakthroughs you made, the person you discovered yourself to be.

This world will try to force you to be the person that is most useful to everyone but yourself. While you lived happily out of a backpack for a month, you will struggle with the materialistic impulses and minor dramas that occupy our days but don't fill up our souls. The stress of our disconnected world will gradually chip away at the sense of serenity that pilgrimage fosters. I've given you much information on how to physically prepare for the Via, but only you can mentally and spiritually prepare yourself for the rigors of pilgrimage and for the return to the world we've constructed for ourselves.

My trips on the Via have been the happiest times of my adult life. For a few days, I understand what it means to be truly free – to be able to go anywhere my feet can carry me, to live by my own sense of time, to do or not do as I choose. And like every pilgrim, upon returning

I have struggled to live my life as the person I was on the Via. From what I have observed, there is only one way to hold on to that better self: to go on pilgrimage again.

I hope you experience the same joy and find whatever it is you seek on the way to Rome.

Buona Via.

April 2019

Part IV

Appendix

11. My Via packing list

Items on my person
- Backpack
- Sunglasses
- Hiking boots
- Hiking outfit (hiking socks, underwear, pants/shorts, t-shirt)
- Trekking poles
- Baseball cap
- Wristwatch

Top pocket of my pack
- **Loose**
  - Headlamp
  - Baby wipes
  - Boot laces
  - Bandana
  - Sunscreen
  - Sunglasses case
  - Hand Sanitizer
  - Headphones (in small case)

- **First aid kit**
  - **In addition to the kit...**
    - Duct tape
    - Extra batteries for your head lamp
    - Emergency whistle
    - Molefoam

- **Laundry sack**
  - Clothes pins (7 of them)
  - Laundry soap packets

Main Compartment

- **Food sack (at the top of the compartment)**
    - Clif bars
    - Picnic lunch or snack
- **Toiletries sack**
    - Shower towel
    - Ear plugs
    - Shampoo
    - Toothpaste
    - Tooth brush
    - Comb
    - Soap
    - Deodorant
    - Prescription medications
    - Ibuprofen
    - Imodium
    - Ambien

- **Electronics sack (next to food sack at the top of the compartment)**
    - Plug adapter
    - Smartphone
    - Phone charger
    - Camera (in small case)
    - Camera charger
    - Memory cards
    - Camera batteries

- **Clothing sack (middle of main compartment)**
    - Hiking pants
    - Hiking shirt
    - Button front shirt
    - Gym shorts
    - Hiking socks
    - Boxer-briefs

- **Cold weather sack (next to clothing sack in the middle of the compartment)**
  - Long underwear
  - Fleece hat
  - Gloves
  - Fleece jacket

- **Sleeping bag liner (in its own compression sack, down at the very bottom of the main compartment)**

- **Sandals (stuffed on either side at the bottom of the pack**

- **Travel day bag (for plane and train rides)**
  - Kindle

Hipbelt pockets
- Washcloth
- Pocket knife

Shovel pocket
- Rain cover
- Rain jacket
- D-ring (clipped to the outside)

Side pockets
- Credential
- Nalgene bottle

Hydration sleeve
- 2-Liter hydration bladder

Money belt
- Cash
- Passport
- Health insurance card

- Travel health insurance card
- Train tickets
- Hotel reservations (if any)
- Plane tickets
- List of contacts, medications, and medical conditions
- Debit card
- Credit card

Pants pockets
- Wallet
- Camera
- Via guidebook pages

12. A few Italian words and phrases

Greeting	Hello	Ciao
	Good morning	Buongiorno
	Good afternoon	Buon pomeriggio
	Good evening	Buonasera
	Goodnight	Buona notte
	Goodbye	Addio
	My name is...	Il mio nome è...
Language	Do you speak English?	Parli inglese?
	I do not speak Italian	Non parlo Italiano
	Can you please repeat that?	Puoi ripetere per favore?
	I'm sorry, I don't understand	Mi dispiace, non capisco
Polite	Thank you	Grazie
	Please	Per favore
	Sir	Signore
	Madaam	Madaam
	Excuse me	Scusami
	I'm sorry	Mi dispiace
	How are you?	Come stai?
	I am good	Sono buono
	I am bad	Io sono cattivo
People	Man	Uomo
	Woman	Donna

	Boy/Girl	Ragazzo/Ragazza
Tourist	Is this the entrance?	È questo l'ingresso?
	Where is the exit?	Dov'è l'uscita?
	Where is the toilet/ bathroom/restroom?	Dov'è la toilette/ bagno / bagno?
Conversation	Yes	Sì
	No	No
	I don't know	Non lo so
Shopping and eating	May I have the bill now?	Posso avere il conto ora?
	How much does it cost?	Quanto costa?
	Chicken	Pollo
	Pasta	Pasta
	Potato	Patata
	French fries	Patatine fritte
	Apple	Mela
	I would like an apple,	Vorrei una mela, for favore
Sleeping	A room	Una stanza
	A bed	Un letto
	Shower	Doccia
	I have a reservation	Ho una prenotazione
	My phone number is...	Il mio numero di telefono è...
	May I leave my bag at the desk?	Posso lasciare la mia borsa alla scrivania?
Weather	What is the weather	Che tempo fa domani?

	tomorrow?	
	Sunny	Soleggiato
	Rain	Pioggia
	Hot	Caldo
	Cold	Freddo
	Pleasant	Piacevole
Directions	Where is...	Dov'è...
	Right	Destra
	Left	Sinistra
	Straight	Dritto
	Backward	A rovescio
	North	Nord
	South	Sud
	East	Est
	West	Ovest
Time	What time?	A che ora?
	What time is it?	Che ore sono?
	It is 14:00 o'clock.	Sono le 14:00.
	Today	Oggi
	Tomorrow	Domani
	Yesterday	Ieri
Numbers	Zero	Zero
	One	Uno
	Two	Due
	Three	Tre
	Four	Quattro

		Five	Cinque
		Six	Sei
		Seven	Sette
		Eight	Otto
		Nine	Nove
		Ten	Dieci
		Hundred	Centinaio
		Thousand	Mille
Via		Pilgrim	Pellegrino
		Bicycle pilgrim	Pellegrino della bicicletta
		I am walking the Via Francigena	Sto percorrendo la Via Francigena
		Yellow arrow	Freccia gialla
		How far is it to the next village?	Quanto è lontano il prossimo villaggio?
		Common Via greeting and farewell	Comune via saluto e addio
Travel		Airport	Aeroporto
		Bus	Autobus
		Train	Treno
		Bus/Train station	Stazione degli autobus / dei treni
		Ticket	Biglietto
		Bus stop	Fermata dell'autobus
		Taxi	Taxi

13. Good resources for learning more about the Via

Viefranciegne.org/en. The official website of the Via, to the extent there is such a thin.

The **Via section** of the Tuscan government tourism website.

Rick Steves' website. His company, Rick Steves' Europe, is probably the best resource of information about traveling to Europe.

Finally, please leave a review of this book on Amazon. These reviews help me improve the information I make available to pilgrims, and if you found this book helpful, you can help your fellow pilgrims by letting them know as well. Buona Via!

About the Author

Ryan Tandler is a pilgrim, author and survey researcher. This is his second book. He has written about the Camino de Santiago in Spain. His most recent book is a memoir about his 130–pound loss.

Made in the USA
Las Vegas, NV
10 May 2023

71857046R00070